CHOOSE
RESILIENCE

CHO✓SE
RESILIENCE

Break Out of Your Comfort Zone
Using the Power of **Emotional Intelligence**

JEN SHIRKANI

First published by Jen Shirkani LLC, Inc.

Copyright © 2017 by Jen Shirkani

First Edition

15 Constitution Drive #1A, Bedford NH 03110

Tel: 603-488-1657

www.chooseresiliencebook.com.

Cover Design: StyleMatters, LLC, info@style-matters.com

Interior Design: StyleMatters, www.style-matters.com

Library of Congress Control Number: 2017904606

Paperback: 978-0-9986122-0-1

eBook: 978-0-9986122-1-8

Audiobook: 978-0-9986122-2-5

Printed in the United States of America on acid-free paper

14 15 16 17 18 19   10 9 8 7 6 5 4 3 2 1

This book is dedicated to my grandmother,
Irene M. Evans
(December 14, 1920–September 21, 2016)

ACKNOWLEDGMENTS

Many wonderful people contributed to this book:

- To Steve Friedlein, thank you for helping me get started and being my constant supporter and encourager and for holding me accountable for writing this book when I wasn't sure that I could.
- Thank you to Suzanne Murray and Rachel Fending of StyleMatters; your professional help in assisting me to organize my ideas and words was invaluable.
- I also want to acknowledge Angela Bearor and Jane Mata for their help and ongoing support. You are both incredible women with a lot of resilience!
- Of course, thank you to Caitlin and Annie for being such wonderful daughters and for being patient with me as I stumble through motherhood.
- I also want to thank Michael J. Fox, Elizabeth Smart, Mary Johnson, Trisha Ballard, Nicole Lorey, and Greg Hawks for their contributions to this book.
- I am incredibly grateful to Sam Matagi for allowing me to share his story in detail. Sam, your resilience is an inspiration to everyone who learns about you.
- Mostly, I want to thank David Bailey. Your love and support remind me every day what really matters in life. I will love you forever.

TABLE OF CONTENTS

*"You never know how strong you are,
until being strong is your only choice."*

—Bob Marley

Introduction

We all make choices every day, but too often, when given the option, we choose to stay comfortable and resist doing things that make us uneasy or seem difficult. We may be easily offended by those who don't agree with us, so we judge and avoid them. We may blame other people or our circumstances for our problems, our unhappiness, or that nagging feeling of discontent with our life.

What I have learned in my years of working with a wide variety of people is that those who are the happiest are not necessarily the luckiest or the most comfortable. The happiest people have faced struggle and hardships, even at times putting themselves in difficult or uncomfortable situations—but have *chosen* to be happy anyway.

They choose to take responsibility for their actions and accept the consequences of their decisions. They understand that they must be willing to adapt to other people's needs, emotions, and perspectives, instead of just interacting with others in the way that feels easiest and most comfortable. They choose to be resilient and thrive instead of deciding to give up and just get by.

These traits are the cornerstones of emotional intelligence (also known as EQ). I have spent my career immersed in the subject of EQ and have seen firsthand all the ways that people become stronger and happier when they start the journey of learning more about themselves and becoming more aware of the impact their behaviors have on others.

For the past twenty years, I have been president and CEO of a boutique consulting firm called Penumbra Group. We provide executive coaching, hiring and selection consulting, and training and development workshops to a wide range of clients, from family-owned businesses to Fortune 50 companies. We work with both U.S.-based and international organizations to increase employee effectiveness through the development of EQ competency.

To get the best results from interactions in my work and personal life, I rely on EQ daily. It helps me recognize my emotional state and reactions, read my audience and the environment I am in, and respond in ways that meet the needs of the people I am with or what the situation calls for, to get the best results from the interaction. Most of the time it works, and when it doesn't, I can usually think back and see how I might have been my own worst enemy.

Both personally and professionally, I have had my own share

of ups and downs over the years, just like everyone else. As I've struggled through tough times and celebrated good times, I've learned important lessons about resilience. I have also experienced the benefits of getting uncomfortable. My intention is to share with you what I've learned, including the ways people can use EQ to be more resilient.

Choose Resilience is for someone like you who wants to learn how EQ can help you become more fulfilled. Resilience is the key to overcoming unexpected difficulties and recovering faster, while growing stronger with each challenge life throws your way. When you push yourself out of your comfort zone, you build your endurance, confidence, and a sense of accomplishment. I will share my own story along the way to illustrate how you might apply the concepts of this book in real and sometimes difficult situations. The goal is to leave you with some new ways of looking at the choices you face, along with tools to increase your motivation, optimism, and stress tolerance. These EQ skills will ultimately build your endurance and put you on the path to greater happiness. I feel honored to be taking this journey with you.

CHAPTER 1

Dark Days

The plunge into darkness came without warning. I hadn't planned for the catalyst that started it all, let alone the whole chain of events it triggered—and I certainly wasn't prepared for the circumstances I suddenly found myself in.

Until that point, I'd never really experienced serious struggle or hardship. My husband and I had been on a trajectory of personal and professional success, and I had come to expect that our reasonably good fortune would continue. I was living my life in a comfort zone, a safe little bubble where everything ran smoothly and I never had to push my own limits. I had no reason to believe that bubble was about to pop or that my course would be significantly altered any time soon. I don't mean to infer that my life was without challenges, but until this point in time, they hadn't felt insurmountable.

Falling Into Darkness

Some of the darkest days in my life began more than a decade ago, when my older daughter, Caitlin, was two and I was pregnant with my second child, Annie. At the time, we were living in Orange County, California, where I had grown up. My husband, Steve, was a salesman in the high-tech consulting industry, and I owned a management consulting and leadership development practice called Penumbra Group. In addition to running my business and preparing for maternity leave, I was caring for a toddler and had just started working toward my master's degree. We hadn't planned on having another child until I'd finished the program, but I was thrilled to be having another baby. Life was busy but good.

Four months into my pregnancy, radical changes rocked both my personal life and the world around me. The disintegration began a few days before September 11, 2001. On the Friday before the planes flew into the World Trade Center, Steve's company laid him off. We spent the weekend trying to figure out what our next step was going to be.

Then, on Monday, at my twenty-week ultrasound, the doctors told us that our baby had a complication with one of her kidneys. They described it as a dilated kidney, likely caused by an obstruction that was prohibiting the kidney from draining and developing properly. At that point, one of her kidneys was double the size of the other. The doctor couldn't tell us how severe the problem was or give us any kind of prognosis—we would have to wait until the baby was born to learn more.

The bubble of my safe and comfortable life had burst! When I woke up on Tuesday, September 11, the safety we had always taken for granted as Americans had also been burst. Terrorists had slipped past all our careful screening systems, infiltrated our airports and our office buildings, and even—through the news we couldn't seem to turn off—invaded our living rooms. As a nation, we realized how vulnerable and unsafe we really were.

Suddenly, it wasn't just Steve and I who had been thrown out of the safe confines of our tidy life; the whole country had been jettisoned out of its comfort zone. Airports, schools, and commercial buildings were shut down. In those establishments that were still open, people felt afraid to gather, wondering where the next terrorist attack might occur.

I had been booked for business travel in the weeks following September 11, but now that terrorists had hijacked three planes, the entire country suddenly felt air travel was too dangerous. Every company that had scheduled people to fly to meetings and conferences said, "Not happening. We're canceling." Steve had just gotten laid off, and three days later, my entire calendar canceled out for the next month. Because I billed only for the time I worked, my income for the foreseeable future vanished.

Within a few weeks the dot-com bubble burst, and job prospects for Steve looked grim. We had lost his company health insurance policy and had to switch to a COBRA plan. To our shock and amazement, the monthly premium was almost as much as our mortgage payment. Because baby Annie had been diagnosed in utero, she was considered to have a preexisting condition. So, unfortunately, reinsuring her under a cheaper plan was impossible.

Annie was born a week early, a tiny five-pound, twelve-ounce bright spot in a very dark period. As the doctors had predicted, she did have a severe kidney defect. One ureter was unsuccessfully attached, which meant her kidney wasn't able to drain properly. If something wasn't done quickly, Annie would become very sick.

We spent the next three months seeing specialists, contemplating treatment options, and functioning on very little sleep. The doctors wanted to remove Annie's defective kidney, which would have involved performing a complicated surgery on a twelve-week-old baby. We trusted them, but we were hesitant. She was still so small, and the surgery would leave her with a long scar slashed across her belly. My heart broke at the thought of my little baby going through that.

After months of indecision and time spent sifting through the choices, we found a surgeon who advised a less-invasive procedure, and we followed this new treatment path with relief. Even without major surgery, Annie was a fussy baby and demanded a great deal of attention. Steve and I had our hands full monitoring Annie's health and taking care of our precious Caitlin, who was surely getting less attention than she deserved.

As consumed as we were with Annie's care, though, we still had to grapple with our financial problems, too. With Steve out of work, we had no choice but to adjust our lifestyle and try to strategize a new employment game plan. Steve was able to pick up a few consulting projects to help out, but the whole technology sector (especially in California) had been wiped out. I had planned on taking some time off after Annie was born, but given our situation, I found myself back to work when she was just five weeks old, patchworking together whatever income I could get. A cloud of uncertainty and anxiety hovered over the country in the aftermath of the attacks, and my clients, large and small, were waiting to see what would happen next.

Yes, Steve and I reacted to the bursting of our comfort zone bubble, but not in particularly creative ways. Rather than coming up with outside-the-bubble solutions to bring us new business, we resisted getting uncomfortable and trying new approaches. Instead, we stuck to our familiar methods for earning income: reading the classified ads, attending the same association networking meetings every month, and maintaining my company's website in the hope that clients would find me online. We clung to the plans we'd made prior to our darkest days and our beliefs about what our life should be like. Shame and pride held us back from letting the people who were close to us know how we were struggling. Those choices kept us further stuck in our own rut, without the support of family or the influx of new ideas and resources they could bring.

Meanwhile, we were draining our savings account and eventually had to borrow money from family. By the following Christmas, we had exhausted our cash flow and our options. This led to a key moment of choice for us: Ask for help from family, friends, or the government via public assistance, or swallow our egos and get temporary jobs.

We chose temporary jobs, and both of us went to work on the sales floor at Nordstrom. Yes, the sales floor. Steve worked during the day, and I worked nights and weekends so I could attempt to operate my consulting practice during business hours.

Although these jobs earned us desperately needed income, I wasn't psychologically prepared to face the circumstances I now found myself in. As an educated woman running my own company, I was mortified that I needed to work a second job to keep my family afloat.

One night while I was working at Nordstrom, a woman walked into my department who seemed very familiar to me. I searched my memory, trying to place her. Did I know her from the gym? From Caitlin's preschool? Then it struck me: We had just met the day before, at an industry networking event.

My next moment of choice hit me straight in the face. I could run and disappear into the stockroom before she saw me, or I could swallow my ego, reintroduce myself to her, and admit that my business was in a slump.

I would *love* to say that I picked the more mature second option, but did I? Hell, no. I followed my first instinct, which was to duck into the stockroom to hide. Shame radiated through my body. I knew that I was being a bit of a coward by avoiding such a terribly uncomfortable situation, but I just didn't have the confidence to admit that my business was in such dire straits that I had no choice but to work a retail job at night. The truth hurt. I fought against accepting my new reality. I certainly didn't want my business colleagues to know.

Although I had found the courage to take a side job, in that moment I cowered in the stockroom, paralyzed by my expectations for my life. I'd gotten stuck in a comfort zone about my identity: I was supposed to be financially well off. I was supposed to have two healthy children. I was supposed to have a happy life with just the usual array of easily solved problems. I had done everything right up until this point, hadn't I? Yet here I was, selling blouses and pants on the night shift. As far as I was concerned, either the universe was very unfair, or I had done something wrong and was being punished with failure. It wasn't Nordstrom that was the issue, it was my inability to understand the larger meaning behind my circumstances. I had a faulty belief system.

I had spent seven years at Nordstrom (all through my education) and had always loved working there. But now my needs had changed completely, and a retail job didn't fit with my ideas about who I was and what my life was supposed to be like. I kept thinking,

- "I should be past this phase in my life."
- "I am a mother of two kids, and I'm supposed to be driving a new Volvo station wagon by now, instead of an old Volkswagen."
- "I should be with my friends who don't have to work. I should be going to the beach, shopping at the mall, and talking about decorating a vacation home."

I had gone to college, waited to have kids until I was in my thirties, and married an older, "stable" man. I really thought I had done everything right, and I felt like I'd been cheated out of the life of my dreams (which I honestly thought I deserved). Throughout my life, I had operated on the belief that if I was good, smart, and diligent enough, I could control my circumstances, and everything would turn out okay. Heck, I thought I would even build the ideal life of my dreams.

Why not? I had seen it happen in movies, and I saw it when I looked across the fence at friends, family, and neighbors. I didn't account for the fact that real life always calls us to grow, and that sometimes the opportunities for growth come in unexpected and undesirable packages.

So I found myself buying groceries with the coin jar money we had previously kept for pay phones and parking meters. I would look at my empty pantry and experience a sickening feeling. I felt like a complete failure. It did not dawn on me that this was real living and that each and every one of us faces hardship in one form or another. I did not yet recognize that no matter how hard we try to stay in our personal comfort zone, life will always find a way to lever us out of it.

What Steve and I did realize was that unless things changed quickly, we would likely have to face another difficult choice: whether to sell the home we loved and move out of Orange County to somewhere more affordable, which would mean leaving my family and support system behind. What had begun as a health crisis had developed into a financial crisis that now threatened to change our entire future.

As financial pressures continued to build, the stress of Annie's kidney condition elevated our tension even further. The doctors believed we would begin to see improved functioning of her kidney within six months after her surgery, so we set up an appointment for a follow-up test when she was nine months old. It was an unpleasant procedure that involved an IV drip, a catheter, and an X-ray every minute for an hour. The medical staff had to restrain Annie to keep her still, and she and I both cried all through that traumatic hour. I moved forward assuming the best, desperately hoping the results would show that the surgery had been a success. I was convinced that I deserved some good news and assured myself that it was forthcoming.

I vividly remember the day the doctor called with the test results. He said, "I am sorry. I was really hoping we would see a difference in the size and function of Annie's kidney by now, but we don't."

I was devastated. We had already put Annie through so much, and now it was apparent that we'd made the wrong treatment decision. I worried about how we would cope with more surgery and how we would survive financially if I had to take more time off work to care for her. It was agonizing to contemplate how we could continue to afford the astronomical health insurance premiums without falling even more behind on our mortgage. The pressure felt enormous.

I hung up the phone and fell on my knees in a complete breakdown. I sat sobbing for a long time, again asking why this was happening to me. What had I done so wrong to have been dealt this punishing blow? I spent the rest of that week in a huge pity party.

- "Why did I have to be the one to have a sick baby?"
- "Why can't my husband be like all the other husbands, with a steady job and benefits?"
- "My sister has three healthy kids, why couldn't I have two healthy kids?"
- "Why did I have to get pregnant when I did? The timing was awful."

- "How am I expected to support our family on an inconsistent self-employed income?"
- "I should be driving a nicer car and going on vacations, like my friends."
- "If we have to move, I won't know anyone. How will I ever get over the guilt of leaving an unhealthy baby in day care?"
- "If we can't sell our house, we'll lose it. We'll have to live in an apartment with college students. What losers."
- "I deserve better. This is not the life I wanted."

I felt like a victim, all alone in my misery. I did not yet know that the hardships I faced were not about cruelty, unfairness, or personal failure; they were an invitation from the universe for me to grow—an opportunity for me to get out of my comfort zone and start to think differently and become my very best self.

A Light Out of the Darkness

I had lost my way. I was bitter and angry. I struggled to make sense of what was happening, until one morning . . . I woke up and immediately started my daily "woe is me" list of worries . . . and then stopped my train of thought.

I reflected on my older daughter, Caitlin. She was a delightful toddler. She had been a steady, sweet passenger on this crazy ride. I thought, "Aren't we lucky that she is so easygoing?" Guilt flooded over me as I contemplated how much of the last year I had spent being absorbed by everything that was affecting *me*. I thought about what Caitlin had been going through, with a distracted mother, a father trying to save his career, and a baby sister who was getting all the attention. Yet Caitlin was a happy, independent little girl who was just loving and supportive.

All I could think was, "What's wrong with me?" I was so angry with myself for being selfish and focusing only on what I thought *I deserved.* My anger toward myself was harsh, but it moved me to a healthier place.

I lay in bed that morning and realized I had another choice to make. I could continue to be negative and angry and unhappy, or I could focus on what I did have. I contemplated the long list of blessings in my life:

- "I have a wonderful, sweet, healthy four-year old."
- "I have an emotionally supportive husband who is a great father."
- "I have a beautiful home with plenty of equity."
- "I have a company, a career, and a college education."
- "I was given a child with medical needs because I am capable of taking care of her. I have access to the best possible treatment and doctors in the country."
- "Although she might have one nonworking kidney, the other one is healthy. And she only needs one to live a normal life."
- "She has no pain associated with her condition. It's a hidden defect, so no one will know about it. The truth is, the odds were much higher that she could have been born with Down syndrome or spina bifida, which are much more serious conditions."

Once I thought through the list, my choice was obvious. I got out of bed a newly determined person. I couldn't believe how motivating it was to see the same circumstances through the lens of positivity and strength.

I shared my new focus with Steve, and together we took back some control in our life. We made a major decision: If I didn't have a solid client contract within sixty days, we would both put our resumes on the market (including out of state) and take the first good job one of us landed. We focused on Caitlin. As far as Annie's health was concerned, we decided that as long as she had no symptoms and a healthy second kidney, we would wait to pursue any additional medical treatments. In the meantime, we agreed to parent her like any other kid and not spoil or coddle her.

Even though our future seemed to be outside of our control, establishing "if–then" plans felt so empowering. It allowed us to take back control of our reactions to events that had been imposed on us. Yes, we'd been roughly shoved out of our comfort zone, but that did not mean we had to give in to chaos. We could choose to be proactive. We created a plan for dealing with our challenges. We could compartmentalize them, face them one at a time rather than letting them overtake us. All of this gave us a greater sense of peace, clarity, and confidence.

Once we took responsibility for our situation and committed ourselves to change, our mood lifted, and things started to fall into place. Four weeks later I got a huge contract from a company I had been diligently prospecting for the better part of a year. It was enough money to support us for six months. Steve decided to enroll in a top-tier college and finish his degree while taking care of the kids (which meant we didn't have to use full-time day care). I got uncomfortable and made the cold calls I had been avoiding. I branched out to network at association meetings where I didn't know anyone. I continued the master's program I had started before I got pregnant. I did not want to go into debt, so I spread the classes out over time, taking them only when I could afford to. It took me four and a half years to complete my degree—but I managed it during one of the busiest and most taxing times of my life, without incurring any student loans.

We Are Stronger Than We Realize

Resilience. Strength, stamina, grit, endurance, recovery, growth, hope. Resilience is built into our DNA. Keep in mind that we are biologically predisposed for it. Too many of us have lost our ability to tap into our resilience because it is a deeply hidden resource. It is there by design for emergency situations, but one thing is required to access it: We must set aside our ego, instead showing vulnerability and humility.

When we're faced with the invitation to leave a comfort zone or we've been thrust out of it unexpectedly, we have a choice to make about how we respond. We can demonstrate humility by becoming grateful for what we have and engage in problem solving. We can strengthen our resolve to make our life better. We need to trust more in our innate human power.

The two biggest barriers preventing us from breaking out of our comfort zone are the uncertainty of the future and the regrets we continue to harbor over choices we made in the past. It's so easy to agonize over thoughts of what we could have done differently. But the fact is, until we release ourselves from self-doubt and recrimination, we limit our capacity to manage our current challenges and opportunities. Once we fully engage in the work of creating positive change in our personal and professional life, our confidence builds with each small success along the way. We draw energy from those successes, which better prepares us to tackle the challenges each new day brings.

In all honesty, I hate this part of my story. For many years I tried to forget it or pretend it didn't happen, and I certainly didn't share it with others. Looking back on it today, I am actually glad I had that experience because of the perspective it has provided me. What I have learned is that we all are capable of managing more than we give ourselves credit for.

I had no idea at the time how blessed I really was. After facing those challenges—and more since then—I know that there is a way to own our thinking and reactions instead of letting them own us. I now see that instead of focusing all my energy on preventing challenges and difficulties in my life, I need to focus on being happy *despite* the challenges and difficulties. Once I started paying attention to how much I had to feel grateful for, I stopped personalizing my circumstances and came to realize that maybe I hadn't done anything wrong at all. Maybe life just happens, and it happens to *everyone*—sometimes in broad daylight, and sometimes behind shuttered windows and locked doors.

Granted, when I find myself in difficult circumstances today, they are no less demanding. But as a result of my struggles, I am better equipped to handle them. When we choose to be resilient, each new challenge we face builds our confidence and brings us a new level of determination to rise above our circumstances, whether they are self-imposed or outside the realm of our control. And you know what? We have the resources and wherewithal to deal with whatever comes our way.

Getting fired or laid off, losing a loved one, going through a divorce, or falling into poor health can really *suck*. Yet each subsequent challenge in our life can teach us new truths and renew our hope. Each obstacle we overcome sets the stage for us to move beyond a struggle and into a new level of understanding about ourselves and who we really are. And those goals we have always wanted to achieve? Sometimes the arrival of unforeseen challenges in our life is exactly what helps us establish and reach them.

Think about a difficult experience you've faced, when you found the strength to overcome the challenge. Ask yourself, "What good has come from surviving that adversity?" If you open your mind, you're likely to find that even in the midst of pain, fear, or loss, you probably experienced at least one of the following:

- the miracle of loving relationships
- a strength born out of weakness
- the courage to do something you've always wanted to do
- a change in your outlook on life.

Take a moment to think about what you learned and gained from your own past hardships when you chose to face them head on. How did they make you better, stronger, wiser? It takes courage to own the positive side of challenge, but when you begin to do so, you regain the opportunity for growth. You discover that the gold is not in the comfort zone; it's in the *confidence zone* . . . but more on that later.

Using Emotional Intelligence to Survive and Thrive

Choosing to face struggle takes some stamina, courage, and resiliency. And you are probably asking, "Where does it come from?" One of my areas of professional expertise is a behavioral science topic known as emotional intelligence, or EQ, and part of my work is helping organizations and leaders be more effective in hiring and motivating others by becoming more socially and self-aware. What I started to realize as I faced my own personal difficulties is that I could leverage the power of EQ to help me overcome them. If IQ is a measure of your intellect, EQ gauges your ability to read a situation involving yourself or others and to respond appropriately. An easy way to operationalize EQ is through what I call "the three *Rs*": *recognize*, *read*, and *respond*.

Recognize

The first of these EQ components is your ability to *recognize* yourself. It involves understanding how you're wired: what your strengths and weakness are, your personality type, your communication style. It's having the emotional self-awareness to recognize when you're in a bad mood and why, to know when you're under stress, and to understand what your triggers are. This depth of information about yourself can be an incredible tool. If you know your level of energy is highest in the morning, you can plan your workday so that you address your most demanding tasks first. If you can tell your spouse, clearly and calmly, why you feel frustrated, you might resolve the problem without an argument.

Read

The second component of emotional intelligence is your ability to *read* people and situations accurately. It's essentially having situational awareness. Reading a situation involves paying attention to people's nonverbal cues, such as body language, and to the layers of meaning behind their words. It requires you to understand what other people might be feeling and to see their point of view. You might draw on this skill when walking into a meeting, using the nonverbal cues to read the mood of the room before anyone has even said a word. Or you might use it to adjust your tone of voice or what you say to someone after they've shared some bad news.

Respond

The final component of EQ is your ability to *respond* to a situation appropriately instead of letting an emotional trigger dominate your behavior. People who pride themselves on being straightforward and speaking what's on their mind might tend to respond in the same way no matter what the situation. Whether they are speaking to their boss or a close friend, they may act in the same direct, outspoken way. With a healthy dose of EQ, however, they are able to read the other person and calibrate their response accordingly. They understand that some people might react better to a gentler, more tactful approach than their standard direct style. When your emotional intelligence is in full force, you take responsibility for the way you respond to a situation, and you adjust your behavior to your audience and your circumstances.

The good news is, there's no secret formula for EQ; with a little effort, anyone can develop a strong emotional intelligence to draw on during the small and big moments of life. Read, recognize, respond. Many of you are already doing this to some degree; this book will help you practice and refine those skills until they become automatic. You can use them to handle those times you've been pushed out of your comfort zone, to make the most of the situation and thrive rather than just survive. They can also be used when you've consciously chosen to break out of your comfort zone to achieve new goals and dreams.

RECOGNIZE   **READ**   **RESPOND**

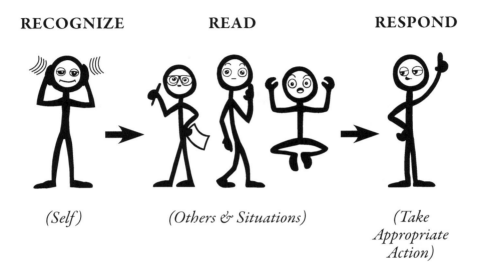

(Self)   (Others & Situations)   (Take Appropriate Action)

What Is the Comfort Zone?

The *comfort zone* is the psychic space we create for ourselves through the routines we engage in and the beliefs we uphold that allow us to feel safe and secure in our daily life—routines like taking the same route to work every day, getting into the same familiar argument with our spouse, or collapsing on the couch in the evening to watch the same TV shows instead of doing something more interesting or productive every so often. It's made up of beliefs like, "No one in my family will get cancer," "This is the only job for me," and "My marriage is bulletproof"—beliefs that you're safe, because nothing truly bad will ever happen to you.

The comfort zone is a "band" of living in which we do the things we are good at or that come easily to us and where the people, places, and activities are familiar. We may not be our happiest or most fulfilled in our comfort zone, but we feel safe. Here are some examples:

- Brian has been working sixty hours a week for the past ten years and is miserable at his job, but it pays the mortgage on his 4,000-square-foot house, and he is good at it, so he keeps on working there.

- Sarah has been married to Hal for twenty years. They have not had sex in two years, and this bothers both of them, but they have not sought counseling and pretend that everything's okay.

- Kevin graduated college, moved back to his hometown, and took a job at his father's accounting firm. It pays him well, and his parents are proud of him, but he is bored at work; he lives for weekends and vacations.

- Rebecca is a stay-at-home mom who prides herself on driving her children to all of their activities, keeping a color-coded schedule of lunches and playdates on the fridge, and hosting themed birthday parties for her kids. She gets everyone everywhere on time in freshly pressed clothes, but she feels a little empty inside.

The comfort zone is a space where you are coasting, feet resting on the bike pedals, not fully engaged or turning the wheels. You might not be unhappy in the comfort zone, but you also are not living the version of your life that meets your fullest potential. Or maybe living in the comfort zone keeps you feeling safe but downright unhappy.

Using EQ to Break Out of Your Comfort Zone

I often say the comfort zone is the enemy of emotional intelligence. When we are unwilling to leave our comfort zone, we often act automatically, without considering what the best response might be. We do what comes easily and most naturally to us, without thinking about the ramifications for ourselves and others. We don't recognize, read, and respond; we simply react.

It's easy to act automatically from the comfort zone rather than use EQ. We're busy. We're overwhelmed. We often live from a place of pessimism, worry, or fear. Consider the following situations, with comfort zone reactions:

- Someone cuts you off in traffic, so you wave your hands, honk the horn loudly, or yell expletives.
- Your spouse forgets your birthday for the third time in seven years, and you declare that one of these days you're going to ask for a divorce.
- Company management institutes a freeze on annual bonuses. You assume it's because they don't value the work that you do, so you start bad-mouthing them in the coffee room.

This is life in the comfort zone. It might be easy to respond without thought, but there are always consequences. Look at the possible outcomes to the previous comfort zone responses:

- After the traffic incident, you are angry for the rest of the day, miss your exit, get pulled over by a police officer for aggressive driving, or get into an accident.

- Your partner, who had never considered ending your marriage, starts wondering whether divorce might actually be realistic, something you really didn't want.
- You were being considered for a promotion but get passed over when word gets out that you were unprofessional and unsupportive of the bonus freeze.

In almost every situation, you have a choice to play things safe or challenge yourself and take a risk. When you use EQ to recognize, read, and respond, it's like pausing long enough to circumvent the gut reaction of the comfort zone that entices you to play it safe. You *recognize* your own emotions (e.g., anger, sadness, fear), and you *read* what's going on for the other people involved.

- You realize that maybe the person who cut you off in traffic was running late to her child's piano recital or was rushing to an emergency.
- You stop to ask your partner what is really going on that's causing him to keep forgetting your birthday . . . and you learn something that makes sense.
- You meet with your boss to ask why the new bonus freeze was instituted, and you learn that it will allow your company to avoid a huge layoff.

By getting good, or even better, at using your EQ, you'll learn to live your life in a way that maximizes opportunity, makes the most of your potential, and helps you create a more amazing, better life.

In Summary—The Choice Is Yours

Choosing a more resilient approach to overcoming challenges will help you become more fully engaged in both your personal and your professional life. The alternative is to remain safe but lukewarm in the comfort zone, not feeling fully engaged, happy, or alive.

What I realized, on that morning when I woke up and finally understood that it was time to take control of my life, was that I had a choice. That same choice is yours to make, too. If you take a hard look and decide that your comfort zone reactions just aren't creating the life you really want for yourself, you can try something different. The following chapters will help raise your self-awareness and give you a strategy for moving beyond behaviors that may be limiting your potential. You can take a risk and find the courage to step out of your comfort zone and instead choose resilience.

CHAPTER 2

How Our Comfort Zone Is Betraying Us

Whatever challenges your very full life holds, it needs to include some comfort, too. It's important to take good care of yourself—so go ahead and settle down with a book and a cup of tea at the end of the day, or pour yourself a glass of wine and turn on the TV, and don't worry about the laundry that still needs to be folded. Rest is important, and comfort is valuable.

The problem comes when we get *too* comfortable, and lose that healthy balance between comfort and risk that keeps us learning and growing. When that happens, the comfort zone becomes a trap, holding us back from becoming our fullest, happiest, strongest selves. In this chapter, you'll learn to recognize what's keeping you in your comfort zone and what you'll gain when you're brave enough to take those first few steps from comfort into courage.

I'll be challenging you to ask yourself some tough questions. If you're willing to do the work, there's so much you can achieve:

- the inspiration to try something you've been afraid to attempt
- the courage to let go of other people's expectations for your behavior
- a new understanding of what will truly make you happy, and what you can release
- a healthier, more rewarding relationship with your children, spouse, family, and friends
- the clarity and motivation you need to become the fullest, best version of yourself.

Maybe you've been struggling lately to break out of a cozy bubble that's starting to feel a little too restrictive, or maybe you're feeling good about the path you're on and energized by the goals you're working toward. Whichever side of the coin best describes you right now, imagine what might happen if you could accomplish just a few of the items on this list. What might your life look like?

What Holds Us Back

Most of the time, fear is what keeps us trapped inside the space that we consider to be safe. We're afraid of the unknown, afraid of losing control, afraid of failing. Uncertainty is scary, and embarrassment feels awful. I get it. But listen carefully, because I want you to remember this: *When you stop taking risks, you lose the opportunity to create the fulfilling, satisfying life you want for yourself.*

I have a friend who had long dreamed of taking dance classes. As a little girl, Jessica had begged for dance lessons, but her mother was a single mom who worked full time and just couldn't get her to classes after school. Jessica felt sad about this for years. She loved to dance at home and at parties, and she always regretted that she had not been able to cultivate her natural talent. Then, one day, Jessica "woke up" and realized that instead of carrying sadness and resentment because her mother had never gotten her to dance class, she could move beyond her frustration and sign up for classes as an adult.

Jessica attended the first class with excitement. But as the next few sessions unfolded, it became clear just how hard it was to teach her body a new language. She had to remember the choreography, tell her body how and when to twist and leap and turn—and do it in front of other, more experienced dancers. She made mistakes, looked awkward, and was definitely out of her comfort zone!

Partway through class one day, Jessica found herself with tears in her eyes, wanting to run out the door and never come back. But she knew that if she did not stick with it, she'd always have to live with the regret that she'd never learned to dance.

It was time for her to make a choice. She could go back to being comfortable with her old exercise routine at the gym, or keep putting herself out there. She could risk looking silly in front of her teacher and peers. She could feel confused and uncomfortable. She could continue with dance classes for the next several months, until her muscle memory and dance vocabulary grew. Or she could stop.

Jessica decided to stick with the classes and continued working through her pain and anxiety. As she overcame each new challenge, she found herself becoming more and more resilient. On each pass across the dance floor, she learned how to focus on learning just a couple of moves rather than trying to master the same long choreography as the more experienced dancers. And when the group engaged in a longer dance at the end of each class, Jessica took pride in the fact that she could follow along for most of it, trusting that over time she would get better and better.

Jessica knew that the only way to grow—or to dance as she'd always dreamed—was to have the courage to play outside of her comfort zone. Each time she left the dance studio, she felt more confident in her ability to take on challenges and learn new things. This self-assurance fueled her other endeavors in life: She started to consider making a career change and took steps to strengthen her marriage, which had gotten stale after twenty years.

Unfortunately, you can't continue to learn and grow if you don't try new things. Without experiencing the discomfort of uncertainty, you won't be able to accomplish those stretch goals you long to achieve: a new career, a fulfilling hobby, the trip of your dreams, a meaningful relationship, you name it. You stay safe and feel secure, yes, but you're unable to create the fullest, richest version of your life that you deserve to have.

You can see the cycle that gets created: The less you test yourself, the more unsure of yourself you will be. When you're unsure of

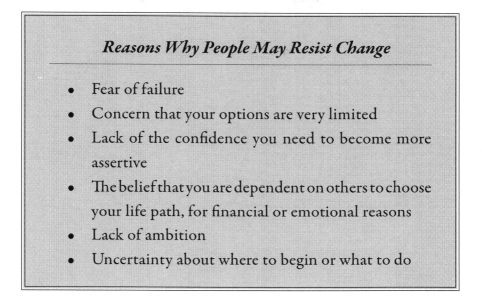

Reasons Why People May Resist Change

- Fear of failure
- Concern that your options are very limited
- Lack of the confidence you need to become more assertive
- The belief that you are dependent on others to choose your life path, for financial or emotional reasons
- Lack of ambition
- Uncertainty about where to begin or what to do

yourself, you'll take fewer risks and resist trying new things, because you're too worried you will fail. You'll lose those opportunities to grow, and feel even less confident in yourself. And so the cycle continues. You may feel confident, because sitting in that narrow, familiar band feels safe. You feel like you can control everything— but it's a false confidence that will fly out the window when an unforeseen event throws you an unpleasant new reality, as it always does. By regularly challenging yourself and choosing to build your confidence muscles, you will become more resilient as real life continues to unfold.

Take a minute to think about the ways that fear might be holding *you* back. These questions are a good place to start:

- What one thing would you do, if you had the freedom or flexibility to do anything?

- Is there something you've been planning on doing for a while but haven't actually put into motion yet?
- What do you enjoy but avoid doing because you think you're not "good enough"?

Maybe you're due for a promotion, but you're afraid to ask in case your boss turns you down. Maybe you've been talking for years about going back to school for your MBA, but you haven't quite found the time to submit an application. Maybe your sister keeps inviting you to join her on her neighborhood soccer team, but you just know you'll trip over your own feet. Whatever you personally have been putting off or holding back from, it's time to break out of that bubble.

Don't worry, you don't have to go it alone. In this chapter and throughout the rest of the book, you'll learn the skills you need to step outside of your comfort zone and into your confidence zone, using EQ as your fuel. Being able to *recognize* your unfulfilled needs or wants and *read* the environment for opportunities and good timing will allow you to *respond* in a courageous way that moves you closer to your goals.

The True Cost of Staying in Your Comfort Zone

Over the years, I've learned that comfort never brings true happiness. Yet comfort is what we're all striving for, isn't it? A nicer house, a better car, a couch that didn't come from IKEA. We tend to measure success in terms of material gains. But take a look at the evidence, and you'll see what a dangerous mistake that can be.

Research has consistently shown that as a society's wealth

increases, so do its rates of depression, anxiety, and suicide. In the United States the number of people taking antidepressants is steadily increasing each year; it doubled between 1999 and 2012.[1] One particularly concerning study found that "urban American women—the most affluent demographic of the study—were the *most* likely" to be diagnosed with depression.[2]

Maybe affluent women have better access to medical care and proper diagnosis than rural or non-American women? However, we in the United States have been swept into a comfort zone of materialism. Technology has caused us to give up many of the things we most crave as human beings, and has left us unhappy in its wake.

Texting is quick and our lives are busy, so we don't call our friends or meet for coffee, and we sacrifice the affiliation and connection we need. We're too busy to cook, so we order takeout food that makes us feel overweight and unhealthy. Just as technology is supposed to make our life more efficient, access to more material stuff has weighed us down with more things to manage. We buy the biggest house we can afford, with a television in everyone's bedroom, and then wonder why no one wants to sit in the kitchen and chat while we cook dinner. We no longer have to chop wood to stay warm or do laundry by hand, but we've lost the satisfaction of hard physical work. Instead, we feel guilty if we don't find time to go to the gym to stay fit.

Modernization and wealth should be giving us more leisure time than ever before, but instead we're stressed and frazzled, with no time to do the things we enjoy. And this seems to be true no matter what phase of life we're in:

- If you've just entered the workforce, you're probably feeling the pressure to make a name for yourself and excel in a tight job market, while trying to figure out what the road map for your adult life should look like.

- If you have children in school, you're juggling your kids' schoolwork and activities with your responsibilities at home and possibly a job as well.

- If you don't have children or if your children are grown, you likely have a busy career and a packed lifestyle. You're keeping your home life organized, making sure to exercise, taking care of family obligations, staying connected with friends, or whatever your to-do list of essentials includes.

- Or maybe you're in the "squeeze zone," trying to care for your aging parents while still taking care of children of your own.

The sad truth is that almost all of us, in all stages of life, are over-committed and stretched too thin. It's not anyone's fault; it's simply where the culture has moved us. It's time to use our emotional intelligence to recognize, read, and respond so we can stop being swept into a familiar but overwhelming and often unsatisfying comfort zone.

A huge part of the problem is that the things we do to stay comfortable are the very things keeping us anxious and unfulfilled. Renovating our kitchen, organizing our closets, and buying that clever new vacuum cleaner from the buy-in-bulk discount superstore haven't led to satisfaction after all. We have to work harder to make the money to afford these things, and then we have to spend the weekend finding space to store all of our stuff. The cycle continues as magazines, TV, roadside billboards, and our neighbors introduce us to the next thing we just *have* to have to perfect our surroundings. The comfort zone has betrayed us.

It's human nature to look outside ourselves, both for the cause of a problem and for the solution. We focus externally and avoid taking control of what happens to us. If we're bored at work, we blame our boss for failing to keep us engaged. If we feel unsatisfied, we think the answer is a nicer house, a better neighborhood, a full social calendar, or an Instagram-worthy vacation.

But the answer is never that simple. During my own darkest days, I longed for a magic bullet to solve my family's problems: a job for Steve, a lucrative project for me, a clean bill of health for my daughter. But as we walk through life, we are shown time and again that external comforts don't soothe an aching soul. The answer to my problems wasn't going to come from a surgeon, my husband, or my clients. What I needed to make me happy had to come from within. It had been with me all along: a feeling of gratitude for all the good things I had been given, and the courage to take ownership of what had happened to me and work to make it better.

So the old adage is true: Money doesn't buy happiness. We already know what *doesn't* make us happy, so what *does*? Waiting for us beyond our comfort zone is a depth of happiness and a sense of fulfillment that cannot be bought or taken in a pill. It doesn't come from possessions or people. It is the sense of accomplishment and the satisfaction you feel when you have overcome adversity, completed a difficult challenge, or taken a big risk and succeeded.

And if you're not ready for major changes right now, that's okay. Even small risks can make your life richer and more meaningful.

How We Hurt Our Children by Protecting Them

The unfortunate fact is that when we cling to our comfort zone, we're not just robbing ourselves of confidence and fulfillment— we're robbing our children, too. If you're a parent, it's natural to want to protect your children. Many of today's parents are from Generation X (born between 1965 and 1981) and grew up when divorce rates were at their highest.[3] They were "latchkey kids," coming home to an empty house after school while their parents were still at work, and they were forced to be self-reliant from a very young age. Often, they might not have had a parent at baseball games or at dance recitals. And when they became parents themselves, they vowed that they would not miss anything in *their* children's life. For the most part, this involvement is a good thing. But, as you might suspect, the comfort zone is a trap to watch out for in this dynamic, too.

As parents, we want our children to be happy and succeed. Just as we can't find true happiness when we stay in our comfort zone, neither can our children. When we rush in to solve their problems, we rob them of the opportunity to face a crisis, get through it, and discover their true capabilities.

Research has shown that today's trend of overly involved parenting has created a rise in anxiety among children and a drop in school performance.[4] In the workplace, many of my clients who are large employers report that the youngest generation of workers are struggling with being autonomous, hearing criticism, and taking responsibility for their actions. Colleges have been accused of grade inflation under pressure from parents who contact professors to challenge grades. When kids aren't encouraged to solve their own problems, they don't gain the confidence they need to be independent. Their parents become even more involved to help them—and the cycle goes on. Good intentions, terrible outcome!

A friend of mine is an admissions counselor at a local college, and he recently interviewed a prospective student, Amy, who was the classic product of this kind of overparenting. Throughout Amy's childhood, her parents had been very involved in every aspect of her life. Her mother volunteered at Amy's elementary school until the day Amy moved to middle school. At that point, mom left her post at the elementary school and moved with her daughter to the new school, so Amy could be assured that her mother was there to step in during any crisis. Unfortunately, given that level of support, there was no need for Amy to become self-sufficient. In fact, when Amy walked into the college admissions interview room, her mother followed. My counselor friend finally asked her to leave the room because she wouldn't stop speaking on behalf of her daughter. Imagine how anxious Amy must have felt being interviewed without the hovering presence of her lifelong safety net, and with no experience of independence to prepare her.

It's important to remember that when we protect our children from struggle, we *deny* them the chance to learn very important EQ skills, including stress tolerance, resilience, and coping strategies. With our children, as with any significant relationship, we have a choice about how we shape our role. When we maintain well-intended control over the actions of others, we hold them back from reaching their full potential. In doing so, we deny them the tools they need to be happy, fulfilled, self-actualized people, too. Don't be afraid to let your children struggle—keep in mind that what you're really doing is giving them opportunities to build their confidence muscles and become the best version of themselves over time.

Perhaps the most important aspect of my message is this: As parents, we cannot worry about being liked by our kids. We are not there to be our children's friend or worry about being the "cool mom or dad." Our job is to let them experience enough struggle to build the critical functional skills they will need in life.

For many of us, parenting becomes another way to look for fulfillment outside ourselves. We often become so involved in our children's life that our identity is woven tightly together with theirs. I understand the temptation—our connection to our children is powerful. But we have to stop and ask ourselves how much involvement is legitimately justified and how much is fulfilling our own desire to be included and needed. Much like retirees feel when they have finally left the workforce, women who have let their children stay safely ensconced in their own comfort zone feel a vacuum when those children grow up and leave home. Their purpose is gone. One more comfort zone betrayal to add to the list.

Seeking Challenge to Build Confidence

Even if you've recognized a little of yourself in these pages and feel motivated to open yourself (and your children) up to new risks and challenges, you may feel uncertain as to how to start. Rest assured, you don't need to shut the door on your comfort zone for good. Instead, the key is to look carefully at the elements of your life and make sure that each day has a healthy balance of comfort and challenge—a chance to stretch yourself, and a chance to rest. I've developed a method that can help you attain that balance. You can role model it for your children and introduce them to the concept as well.

Imagine two scales from 1 to 10. One moves from easy to challenging, and the other moves from uninteresting to interesting. Make a list of the activities that fill your days, and rate them on the two scales. Odds are, the things you find challenging or uninteresting are the things you avoid or dread doing. The things that you find interesting or easy are likely things you look forward to doing. Lay the scales on top of each other to make four quadrants (uninteresting/easy, uninteresting/challenging, interesting/easy, interesting/challenging), and start tracking in a given week the ratio of time you spend in each.

There is a sweet spot between the uninteresting and interesting, the easy and challenging. If you are biasing your time and effort toward the interesting and easy zone and avoiding anything uninteresting or challenging, you are likely living in a comfort zone bubble. And I know it's tempting to think that if you can do the interesting and easy the majority of the time, you will also be engaged and happier. Not so fast. My point is that you should be slowly pushing yourself toward the interesting but challenging work to be a fully realized person, with the confidence and happiness that brings.

The Quadrant Model of Engagement

	EASY	CHALLENGING
UNINTERESTING	**DISENGAGEMENT ZONE** Things you can do without thinking about it. They require little energy or effort and usually don't take long to complete.	**DISCOMFORT ZONE** Things that are either physically or mentally difficult but don't provide any immediate fulfillment once completed.
INTERESTING	**COMFORT ZONE** Things that you can do with ease but enjoy and that keep you mentally engaged.	**CONFIDENCE ZONE** Things that require both physical and mental energy. These tasks generally take longer to complete but provide a deep sense of accomplishment.

The Disengagement Zone

We find ourselves in the disengagement zone when things that used to be interesting have lost their appeal. We still do them, either because we have to or because we have fallen into a rut and haven't realized that we are just going through the motions, bored, or unchallenged. Many of the activities that fall into this quadrant are the necessary but unpleasant tasks that are just part of life, like paying the bills, cleaning the bathroom, or filing your weekly sales report (although the quadrant assignments are subjective—some people enjoy bill paying and cleaning!).

The Comfort Zone

The activities that put us in the comfort zone are the things that require the least amount of energy but keep our interest. We can do them with ease, and they leave us feeling relatively satisfied. Although many of us strive to spend as much time in this zone as possible, it is important to remember that the tasks in this quadrant often require only superficial effort, and they might not be very productive, depending on whether they fall into the category of self-care or self-indulgence. They may feel good for a short time, but that glow wears off eventually, leaving us feeling unfulfilled. Comfort zone activities are different for everyone—eating a favorite dessert, watching a reality TV show, shopping at the mall, going on a beach vacation, or something else.

The Discomfort Zone

This zone is filled with activities that feel more difficult, because they stretch us but aren't enjoyable. We slog through them, because they drain our energy reserves and generally take longer to finish. Even though these tasks may not be fun, they do come with a solid sense of accomplishment when completed, because the time spent in the discomfort zone is productive. Your discomfort zone activities might include planning a presentation, cleaning out your closet, or finally replying to a difficult email (again, it depends on your personality, strengths, and interests).

The Confidence Zone

To complete the tasks in the confidence zone successfully, you must be fully present. There is no coasting through these activities—they demand your full attention, but they also provide a high degree of satisfaction. There will be times in this zone when you question yourself and wonder whether you can complete the activity or are doing a good job, but when your motivation is aligned correctly, this is the path to a fully realized life. The work you do in this quadrant makes you a highly productive and fulfilled person. You might be in the confidence zone when taking on a new role at work, training for a 5K, or learning a new language.

An Example: My Personal Chart

To get you thinking about the kinds of things that might end up on your chart, I've provided my own as an example. These are my personal activities and the way I categorize them, on the basis of my values. You might add some of the same activities to your chart, but for you they might fall in different quadrants, depending on your personal definitions of easy, challenging, uninteresting, and interesting.

Jen's Quadrant Model of Engagement

	EASY	CHALLENGING
UNINTERESTING	**DISENGAGEMENT ZONE** Taking out the trash Designing presentations Making dinner Responding to email Booking travel Filing paperwork Watching TV	**DISCOMFORT ZONE** Working out Helping my kids with homework Creating business proposals Traveling for business Writing blog content Doing research Parenting my teenagers
INTERESTING	**COMFORT ZONE** Visiting with friends or family Bookkeeping Babysitting Watching movies Doing jigsaw puzzles Catching up on social media Shopping	**CONFIDENCE ZONE** Volunteering and doing pro bono work Doing executive coaching work Giving keynote speeches Attending networking events Traveling for leisure Parenting my teenagers (yes, it's in both zones for me!)

People often linger between the disengagement and comfort zones, because it is alluring to stick with what we perceive as easy. When we move away from the easy to attempt things we find challenging, we feel unskilled or unqualified, so we may retreat to the familiar and comfortable. Research and theory might even seem to support this. The Gallup Organization's "strengths movement" argues that when employees are encouraged to focus on their strengths in the workplace, their productivity increases, and they are more satisfied with their job.[5]

As an executive coach, however, I've often worked with people who have overrelied on their strengths to the point that they've become weaknesses. It's not uncommon for people to build a successful career on their talents, only to plateau or, worse, struggle to meet performance expectations because they couldn't adapt to a changing environment and shifting demands. If we concentrate too heavily on our strengths, we can find ourselves stagnating and get just plain bored.

The reality is that we can't spend 100 percent of our time in any of these four quadrants. Yes, the confidence zone is where you'll find fulfillment and happiness, but it's also physically and emotionally challenging to be there. You can't stay in that zone indefinitely. You need to move back to the easy side of the chart to regroup. When you're refreshed, you can tackle the difficult tasks again.

The Zones in Action

Most worthwhile activities start out in the discomfort zone, feeling difficult and unpleasant. Imagine a child learning to play the piano. She might start in the comfort zone as she learns "Chopsticks," but as the lessons become more difficult, she moves quickly to the discomfort zone. You can practically observe the drudgery she feels in preparing for that weekly piano lesson. As parents, we often have to require, beg, threaten, or reward our children to practice. But things change for many children once they master a more difficult song or learn how to read music. They move to the confidence zone as they begin to enjoy the feeling of accomplishment, and it fuels their desire to learn more. Ultimately, if playing music is motivating to them, they become lifelong musicians.

In many ways, just having awareness of the zones and where you are in them is enough to get you started. In my own life, there have been periods when I was so tired, traveling like crazy and just trying to make it through the week, that the last thing I was thinking was, "How do I challenge myself today?" I was just head-down, powering through my days. I didn't have the time to ponder my fear of change or contemplate what I needed in my life to feel fulfilled. I was surviving, but I wasn't truly happy.

I'm sure you've been through times like this, too, when it feels like the very best you can do is to keep treading water and try to stay afloat. You're firmly planted in the discomfort zone. Understanding that can be helpful, because ahead of you lies the confidence zone. Maybe you don't have the time to focus on living your most fulfilled life right now. You can choose a goal or two to work toward that will help move you from discomfort into confidence. You owe it to yourself to take time to evaluate what you are doing and how it makes you feel.

Over time, as I began to consider how I cycle through my zones, I discovered that the high of the confidence zone energized me to get through the things I needed to do in the discomfort zone. For example, I love speaking to groups about EQ. It's challenging and exciting, and it puts me squarely in my confidence zone. But I can't show up at those speaking engagements unless I write the proposals and book the travel, which fall in my disengagement and discomfort zones. I need to spend time in my comfort zone to regroup at night and on the weekends, but then I need to move back up to the discomfort zone. There's no way to have one quadrant without all the others, and too many people quit when things get hard in the discomfort zone, instead of holding on until they make it into the confidence zone.

The key element that keeps us moving through these quadrants is *motivation*. The fulfillment you get from your achievements in the confidence zone will inspire you to knock out the tasks in those other zones so you can get back to what you love. Sometimes it takes me twenty hours of travel just to speak to a group for ninety minutes—but those ninety minutes are so worth all the hours spent on planes and in rental cars. That's what keeps me moving through all the other zones. I want to get back into the confidence zone, but I know the only way to get there again is to go back and hit all the other zones. I'm sure you have your own motivator, the activity that gives you that rush of confidence and satisfaction. Let that be the "carrot" that keeps you moving through the other quadrants.

It is also important to note that the activities on this chart are in flux. As I move from the discomfort zone to the confidence zone, eventually the things I once found challenging may get easier. The things I found interesting may start to bore me. That's why we must always be reaching toward the challenging side of the quadrant model, progressing as we learn and grow. Being in the confidence zone does not require that you chase a big dream; you can be very fulfilled by doing one challenging thing every day.

Challenge Your Instinct to Stay in Control

When we feel our comfort zone is in peril, it is a very common reaction to lock down on the things we *can* control. We avoid the discomfort zone and its unknown conditions by attempting to direct tasks and people. Sometimes, when we're under pressure, we lean more heavily on our strengths because it feels good and it seems safe.

A friend of mine, Jackie, worked for many years as a vice president of human resources and a personnel relations attorney. Jackie was extremely gifted and deeply knowledgeable about every legal issue that crossed her desk. She was also a well-regarded interviewing and hiring manager. Jackie consistently assembled a highly qualified staff of project managers who were capable of managing themselves, as well as the divisions for which they were responsible.

Despite her confidence in the people she brought on to her team, Jackie was known for poring over the minute details of every project they worked on. She was a micromanager, stuck in her comfort zone of personal perfection in every word that she documented, every piece of correspondence she reviewed, and each procedure her team executed. As a result of her deep-seated need to achieve perfection, she never made decisions within a reasonable time frame, and her projects were almost never accomplished on deadline. Her need for perfection became a constant roadblock.

Over time, her unwillingness to move into her discomfort zone eroded her credibility and the respect of her peers and her direct reports. Her inability to venture (even slightly) from her "zone of perfection" put constraints on the performance of everyone in her department. After years of tolerating Jackie's grip on projects and people, senior management finally felt the benefits no longer outweighed the problems created by her management style, and they reassigned her to a position as an individual contributor, essentially demoting her. Her years as a leader with diverse management responsibilities had come to an end. She no longer had the benefits associated with a support staff.

Recently, Jackie told me that she wishes she had opened her eyes to the many ways her perfectionism was holding her back while she had the opportunity to initiate change on her own. In her interactions with her employees, she had a choice to make: involve herself in every little detail, or have more faith in her employees and let go of some control. She perpetually chose the former, justifying her decision by telling herself, "This project is too important. Next week I'll delegate more," and, "I'll give him more responsibility once I can really trust him." But the reality is, people make mistakes, and everyone will let you down at some point. The only way for Jackie to grow—and to help her employees grow—was to take the risk and give her team more responsibility. If she had been able to move into the discomfort zone, she likely would have eventually adapted into the confidence zone—and her career would have progressed quite differently.

I have my own version of Jackie's story. Before Annie was born, when I just had Caitlin, I traveled twice a month on business. Before every trip, I would plan the meals for Steve to cook while I was away and go to the grocery store to buy all the ingredients. I'd lay out outfits for Caitlin to wear the days I was gone—one for each day, in a neat little row with a top, bottoms, underwear, and socks. If I were leaving for three days, I would prepare three little outfits. When I got home, the meals had been eaten and the outfits had been worn;

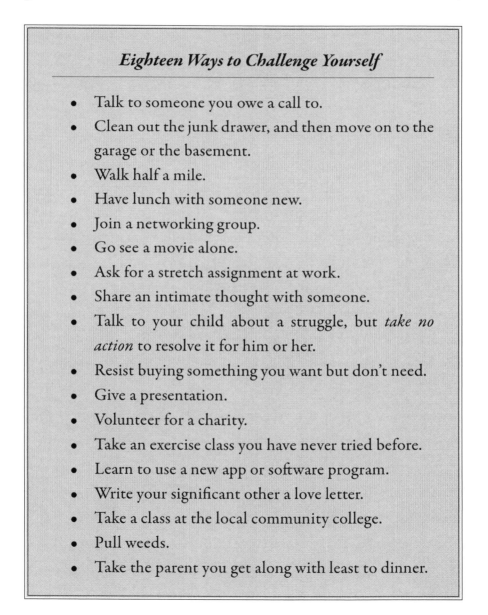

Eighteen Ways to Challenge Yourself

- Talk to someone you owe a call to.
- Clean out the junk drawer, and then move on to the garage or the basement.
- Walk half a mile.
- Have lunch with someone new.
- Join a networking group.
- Go see a movie alone.
- Ask for a stretch assignment at work.
- Share an intimate thought with someone.
- Talk to your child about a struggle, but *take no action* to resolve it for him or her.
- Resist buying something you want but don't need.
- Give a presentation.
- Volunteer for a charity.
- Take an exercise class you have never tried before.
- Learn to use a new app or software program.
- Write your significant other a love letter.
- Take a class at the local community college.
- Pull weeds.
- Take the parent you get along with least to dinner.

everything was good, and Mommy was happy. Then, as you know, I had a second child.

Even though I followed the same routine when Annie was a toddler, she had no interest in wearing anything I had laid out for her. By then, Steve was a part-time student and a full-time dad, which meant I had to expand my business and take on more clients. Suddenly, I found myself with two young children, traveling a lot more than I had been, and trying to keep up with everything else going on in my life. This had not been my plan, but there I was before each trip, totally stressed out. Not only was I getting my work prepared and myself packed, I was also running around to get everything ready at home for when I was gone. After a long week of working with a client in another city, I would come home and find that none of the food I bought had been eaten and none of clothes I laid out had been worn. Seeing that, I would lose my temper every time. I think we all dreaded the day I got home and performed my critical review of the week's activities (or lack of them).

Then, one day, sitting on a plane, I was looking forward to going home but also could feel a knot in my stomach thinking of what I might find on my arrival. Using my EQ, I started *recognizing* my growing anxiety. I finally asked myself why I was getting so worked up. It was a light-bulb moment. I realized that it was crazy to expect that while I was away, everything at home was going to run according to *my* plan.

As the plane began its slow descent, I made a choice to only see good things when I got home. When I walked in the door, I found two happy kids who were fed and bathed. It didn't matter that the meals they ate were out of a box instead of home cooked, or that they hadn't worn matching clothes, or that the lawn hadn't been watered. I finally said to myself, "That has to be good enough. The house didn't burn down, and my family is happy and healthy and alive."

As I reflected on why I had been so controlling, I realized that deep down I felt like the way the household ran while I was gone was somehow a reflection on me. I felt guilty about leaving my kids and was worried that if they went to school all disheveled, people would think, "Can you believe Jen? She's so focused on her career that she leaves those little kids and travels all the time." I was so caught up in how people perceived me, whether I was the kind of mother I was "supposed" to be, that I was making my whole family unhappy, including myself. It was never my plan to be the primary breadwinner in my family (especially when I had young children), but that was the reality of my situation. It was up to me to choose to make the best of it.

And I hadn't been giving my husband any credit. Granted, I gave him no responsibility, but I also gave him no credit. He was a great dad, and he needed to be allowed to parent in his own way. I needed to give him the opportunity to prove he could handle being alone for four days with two young children quite competently—which he could. I had to learn to lean on him.

Eventually, I got good enough at stepping into my discomfort zone when I traveled that I no longer worried about going to the grocery store before a trip. Steve had money, he had a car, and he could figure it out. I didn't worry about laying out clothes for the children—they had drawers full of clean clothes, and they would figure it out. I stopped arranging for day care on the days I was gone and Steve had class; he had the same list of sitters I did, and *he could figure it out*. As uncomfortable as it was, especially the first few times I did it, it freed me up so much that the choice to let go of what happened when I was gone became easier. For our sake and for the people we care about, we need to start asking ourselves why we have this insatiable need to micromanage, whether at work or at home.

This is a trap a lot of us fall into. But don't worry: It's not that hard to avoid. When you're consistently doing something that causes pain for you or the people you care about, take a quiet moment to reflect and recognize the real reasons behind your actions. Ask yourself, "What is the belief system that is keeping me trapped in my comfort zone?" So often, the answer is guilt, or a false idea about who we are supposed to be, which may not match up very well with who we truly are or want to be.

I justified my controlling behavior by telling myself that if failed to take care of something, it would fall on me to fix it. For example, if Steve didn't run to the dry cleaner, I would have to do it when I got home. If he didn't do the laundry, I would have to take care of it. I was just trying to save myself the extra work. But as you can guess, when we are willing to take responsibility for things, people let us. This becomes a self-perpetuating cycle, and we never free ourselves up from things we shouldn't be doing. And what's more, we never require other people to be responsible for themselves and the consequences of their actions (or inaction).

In Summary—Don't Be a Frog

You might have heard the parable of the boiled frog.[6] The theory goes that if you drop a frog into a pot of boiling water, it will jump right back out. But if you put it in a pot of tepid water and very gradually raise the temperature, it won't realize the increasing danger it's in because the change is too gradual. I have felt at times just like a frog being boiled, and perhaps you have, too. Some heat is okay—it means we are stretching and growing and allowing ourselves to struggle. The key is to recognize when it's getting too hot and we have been waiting too long to make decisions or important choices that would improve our life.

To make things more complicated, others are sometimes in the pot with us. I remember times in my marriage when—to use the frog metaphor—I would ask Steve, "Is it getting too hot in here?" and he would respond, "Not for me." Those times were another moment of choice: go along with my partner and stay in a little longer, or blow the whistle and jump out now. The decisions we have to make are not simple or obvious, and it might seem easier to delay or avoid them and just stay in that comfort zone. Sometimes we even hang on to the leg of other frogs to keep them from leaving us alone in the pot, but in the end, we both know that's not the right choice either.

By working hard to take some uncomfortable steps to be more daring, you will also help yourself be more confident and strong. You will learn things about yourself you never knew and find ways to rediscover meaning and happiness from within, so you aren't popping Xanax to stay calm or sleepwalking at work. If you are willing to stretch yourself into the discomfort zone just a little more each day, you can overcome struggle and difficulties to reach your fullest potential. In the next chapters, I will share with you the techniques I have used throughout my life to overcome challenges and reach my goals. They are effective and relatively easy to implement, and they can work for everyone, including you.

Endnotes

1 Elizabeth D. Kantor, Colin D. Rehm, Jennifer S. Haas, Andrew T. Chan, and Edward L. Giovannucci, "Trends in Prescription Drug Use Among Adults in the United States From 1999–2012," *JAMA* 314 (2015): 1818–1830.

2 Sebastian Junger, "How PTSD Became a Problem Far Beyond the Battlefield," *Vanity Fair,* June 2015, http://www.vanityfair.com/news/2015/05/ptsd-war-home-sebastian-junger.

3 W. Bradford Wilcox, "The Evolution of Divorce," *National Affairs,* Fall 2009, http://nationalaffairs.com/publications/detail/the-evolution-of-divorce.

4 Abilash Gopal, "Helicopter Parenting Has Given Birth to a Generation of Entitled Victims," *Huffington Post,* April 12, 2016, http://www.huffingtonpost.com/abilash-gopal-md/helicopter-parenting-has-_b_9657534.html.

5 "Gallup Created the Science of Strengths," Gallup, https://www.gallupstrengths-center.com/Home/en-US/About.

6 "Boiling Frog," Wikipedia.org, https://en.wikipedia.org/wiki/Boiling_frog.

CHAPTER 3

Making the MOST of Your Exit Strategy

When we choose comfort over our EQ, we react from an instinctive place. When we use our EQ instead, we have the tools we need to cope calmly and confidently with the challenges we face. The skills I draw on regularly—and that I will teach you to use to sharpen your EQ and move successfully through the four quadrants—make up what I call the MOST model of resilience. Its three pillars are **M**otivation, **O**ptimism, and **S**tress **T**olerance.

The MOST model will help you when you're faced with major life challenges (e.g., grieving a loved one's death, losing a job, or

51

even sending a child off to college). It's a guide for achieving goals at work and in your personal life, helping you stay engaged and energized on a daily basis. When you use the MOST model, you'll find that you are calmer and less anxious, and you'll build the confidence you need to move out of your comfort zone and into your confidence zone. It will ensure that you don't get stuck in the disengagement zone, too.

The beauty of the MOST model is that it's versatile. It will help you address whatever problems you may be struggling with or goals you're striving to attain. When you are brave enough to let go of your comfort zone and trust your emotional intelligence, you'll be surprised at how much you can achieve. Whether you'd like to lose weight, find a new job, strengthen your marriage, become a better parent, or improve your performance at work, emotional intelligence skills and the MOST model are effective tools to get you there. Building your emotional intelligence will help you face whatever life throws at you with grace and confidence.

Even though my message is about achieving success and finding ways to overcome difficulty or boredom in your life, I also want you to know that I didn't magically overcome the difficulties of my early married life and live happily ever after. I had a strong drive to be successful and confident, and I placed a lot of pressure on myself to achieve my goals—but at the same time, I had a husband who still needed to feel like a man. He needed more than to just stand in the shadows of my success. It's a delicate dance to push through fear and reach your zone of strength without others feeling threatened. It probably shouldn't be like that, but it is. Having the EQ skills to read your environment and know when to accelerate and when to coast is vital to striking a healthy balance between your own achievement and your connections with others.

The last six years have not been easy for me. I have faced another financial crisis, business failures, and, sadly, after eighteen years together, the end of my marriage to Steve. The biggest challenge in creating an exit strategy (from either a comfort zone or a significant life challenge) is accepting responsibility for overcoming the circumstances of your dilemma. That's not the same as blaming yourself; it's about empowering yourself and choosing resilience. Once you take ownership for your life, everything can fall into place. You will be rewarded with the joy of gratitude, growth, and positive change.

People are hardwired to value safety, but avoiding everything that feels uncomfortable makes us selfish, because it ultimately puts our needs above others:

- We avoid visiting aging or sick relatives because it is difficult to see them that way.
- We don't volunteer our time to charities that make us sad.
- We avoid traveling to new places because we are afraid of being in unfamiliar territory.
- We don't go to restaurants alone because we are embarrassed.
- We stay in unhealthy relationships longer than we should because we fear being alone.
- We divorce instead of doing the hard work to save our marriage because it's difficult.

- We stay in jobs and careers that don't fulfill us because finding a new job is too challenging.
- We avoid saying what's on our mind because we want to avoid conflict.

Whenever we find that we're staying in our comfort zone out of fear or avoidance, we need to formulate an *exit strategy*—a permanent change to our philosophy and our responses. The key isn't necessarily to exit your comfort zone all at once; rather, you can make a series of small adaptations that ultimately rewire your intuitive and automatic responses so that you look beyond the easy and comfortable solutions. Gradually, you can become more willing to take on risk, try new things, and pursue your goals. This will help you build a rich life of challenge and fulfillment, resulting in increased pride, self-confidence, and happiness.

Make the MOST of Your Exit Strategy From the Comfort Zone

To successfully move through the four quadrants of the Engagement Model, we need to draw on the skills of *motivation*, *optimism*, and *stress tolerance*. I have found these three EQ skills in particular to be the most valuable for people who want to achieve the confidence zone.

Let's take a look at how each of the three skills that make up the MOST model can establish the basis for a significant comfort zone exit strategy. We will look at each skill in greater depth in the chapters that follow.

Motivation

By definition, motivation is "a propensity to pursue goals with energy and persistence, even despite setbacks."[1] A willingness to take action to help ourselves (instead of waiting helplessly for someone to save us) is a foundational hallmark of those who survive hardship and end up stronger. This self-induced motivation results in resilience and a desire to continue overcoming obstacles. Most people who demonstrate motivation also understand the underlying reasons for their actions. For me, during Annie's health scare, my motivation was obvious: to keep her as healthy as possible. But even when I'm not in crisis, I am motivated to take on challenging situations because they keep me feeling alive and bring me closer to achieving my goals. I might stretch my comfort zone to

- share my knowledge with others to help them grow
- outperform my competition so I can make a healthy living for my family
- learn a new skill, activity, or philosophy to enjoy the rush and satisfaction of growth
- do things for other people so I can make a lasting contribution to my community and the world I live in.

For all of these reasons and more, I stay motivated to overcome difficult situations when my back is against the wall. To achieve all you're truly capable of, it is important that you find out what really motivates you. Easy answers like "I want to be the CEO" or "I want to be rich" won't keep you on task when the going is tough. You'll need to do some real soul searching to determine what you're willing to work for and what your motivations are. What is *really* in it for you if you choose to take more risk and get very uncomfortable?

Motivation gives you the drive and the energy to push into your confidence zone; it is the energetic feeling you have in your body and the determined thoughts that filter through your mind. It's the desire to accomplish something and knowing why you want to accomplish it.

People don't often spend the time to determine where their motivation truly stems from. Maybe their parents influenced their goals ("Good kids like going to school") and their decisions about what to avoid ("Don't choose a career for the money; that's greedy"). Although we sometimes think such external motivation will be enough, actual behavior modification has to be self-motivated.

In my consulting practice, I once worked with a leader who had concerns about one of his employees. The employee, Carl, wanted to advance to a management role. He had first expressed his interest in being promoted about six months after his hire date. He didn't have any management experience, seemed to enjoy working autonomously, and was easily annoyed by peers who interrupted his work flow. My client had a hard time understanding why Carl wanted to be a supervisor. When asked, Carl's reply was always, "I want a promotion. I would like to run a department." It took several meetings to finally uncover his true motivation for wanting a promotion: When Carl was growing up, his father had taught him that non-management employees were disposable. Yet Carl's skill set and interests were poorly suited to the demands of a management role. He hadn't considered whether the job would make him happy; he was just blindly pursuing the goal set by his dad. A promotion to management very likely would have made him miserable.

If your motivation is based on someone else's expectation, you're less likely to make a long-term commitment to change. However, when you are driven by an innate, authentic desire, there's a good chance you will stick with your efforts and do the hard work required to accomplish your goals.

Some Questions to Ask Yourself to Determine What Motivates You

- What activities make you feel the most productive?
- What accomplishments are you most proud of?
- Who in your life would benefit if you overcame an obstacle?
- What traits were you born with that you feel are your best attributes?
- If you could do one thing for a whole year without any restriction, what would it be?

Optimism

Motivation gives you the energy, determination, and focus to take that first step out of the comfort zone. As you move through the journey, however, you will undoubtedly face challenges to your motivation. That's where the second step out of the comfort zone comes in: optimism—a mind-set that everything is going to turn out okay. More than okay, in fact!

Optimism is the belief that the best—that which you strive for—can happen, instead of the worst. Whereas motivation gets you started, optimism helps you persist. When you cultivate optimism, you will be able to move through setbacks rather than allowing them to defeat you, because your whole being will remain lighter and more hopeful. Your positive belief system can carry you through the rough patches. Let's compare that with pessimism—the belief that the worst will happen, that things won't work out well or live up to your expectations. Pessimism will throw water on the fire of your motivation faster than you can say, "EQ."

Optimism as defined in the MOST model is not passive. It's the belief that you can move beyond your current condition, accompanied by the willingness to do the work it takes to get there. It acknowledges that you have the power to change your own circumstances. Think of it this way: If I wish to win the lottery, simply praying to win will not be enough. I have to go and buy a ticket. Good thoughts do nothing for you without action.

The key to this kind of healthy optimism is your ability to do a reality check: to see a situation for what it is, not what you may want it to be. It means letting go of what you wish were true, so that you can accept things as they actually are. When you do this, you take back a measure of control over your own life, and you can begin to change your circumstances. The belief that good things can happen gives you the faith you need to take those first scary steps into your discomfort zone and keep powering through until you get to your confidence zone.

This realistic optimism applies to our expectations of others as well, whether they are our spouse, our parents, our children, or our boss. Oftentimes we want to see some new behavior in someone, so we tell them what we want them to change . . . and every time they fail to do so, we get frustrated and annoyed. I am a firm believer that people can change and adopt new behaviors—but not if they're only motivated to please someone else. True change is usually gradual and doesn't require a wholesale transformation in temperament, personality, or values; those things are pretty fixed. So most of the time, when it comes to other people, what you have been seeing is what you'll continue to get.

I have a friend who is unhappy with her husband. Although he has some good traits, he can't keep a job, prioritizes himself above the family, and is a chronic liar. He has been this way for twenty years. But instead of seeing him as he is, my friend wakes up every day thinking, "Today is the day he will be responsible, honest, and selfless." And every day, when he fails to act that way, she is heartbroken and furious. I love her optimism, but you can see how it borders on delusional.

She is faced with a choice: see her husband as she desperately wants him to be (which keeps the burden exclusively on him to change), or see him for who he actually is. If she sees things more realistically, that means she also has to make another choice: make the best of things, or make a change. Every day he doesn't live up to her vision of how he should be, she hates him for it. It has become such a toxic cycle, filled with resentment and name-calling, that it has torn the family apart. They find themselves in a stalemate over who should change first.

I have had a similar kind of experience with my mother. Over the years, I have put unfair expectations on her and then judged her negatively when she didn't meet them. I clung to an idealistic image of what a mother, wife, and grandmother should be. After years of frustration and disappointment, I finally understood that I needed to make a choice to stop being a dreamy-eyed optimist and instead see my mother (and, more important, appreciate her) for who she was and the effort she did make. I realized that it was really unfair for me to expect her to become someone she has never been and then resent her for failing to do so. Over the years, she sensed my continual judgment of her, which put her on the defensive with me (and sometimes the attack) and only strained our relationship further.

After a particularly difficult series of interactions, I spent some time in self-reflection. I asked myself why my mother was upsetting me so much. I dug deep into my own emotions, motivations, and values. I had to ask myself to what extent my judgment of my mother reflected how *I* wanted to be as a mother, as if my definition of "good" was the only definition. I had made the incorrect assumption that my mother and I had the same capabilities and motivations. We didn't, and I had to understand that she had good reasons for being who she was.

I came to the conclusion that if I wanted a relationship with my mother, I had to accept the person she is. Once I approached her with right-sized optimism, I was able to let go of the negative cycle of hope, judgment, and continual disappointment. As a direct result, we have a happy relationship today.

A healthy optimism allows you to assess the present situation and move outside the confines of your preconceived viewpoints, ideas, options, and reasons to find the positive in what *is*. When you're in the middle of a crisis, each day may be filled with anxiety and dread, and it can be tough to keep going. Having optimism about yourself, your abilities, and the day ahead of you will get you out of bed and give you the stamina you need to persevere. Optimism gives you hope and reminds you that success is possible even against strong headwinds.

Stress Tolerance

Now it's time to talk about stress. If you have been pushed unwillingly out of your comfort zone and into your discomfort zone, there is no doubt that you are experiencing stressors. We all face stressors from everyday life: issues at work, conflicts at home, the pressure to earn a living and pay bills, the need to keep up with all our commitments.

Although stress is an expected part of life, extra stressors are the challenges that will inevitably come up when you try to do something new or different; they are the obstacles you will need to overcome on the way to achieving your goals. Take a look:

Common Stressors in Everyday Life

Situation	Stressors
You choose to end an unhappy marriage.	Reduced income, legal costs, arguments with your ex, relocation to a new home, strain and fatigue from being a single parent, loss of friends
You volunteer to be president of the neighborhood association or the parent–teacher association.	Complaints from the individuals you represent, lack of funding, a natural disaster that damages the neighborhood or school, loss of time
You take a promotion at work.	Added hours and responsibility as you adapt to a new team and increased deliverables, the pressure of learning new tasks, self-doubt about whether you'll succeed in your new role

Facing the decision to end my marriage was very scary. I worried so much about my kids and how they would be affected by a divorce. I worried about Steve and how he would do on his own. I didn't know how I would be able to adapt to life as a single mother and the change in my identity. Before I made my final decision, I pondered whether the stress of divorce might be worse than the stress of staying unhappily married, and by using my EQ, I was able to keep a keen sense of the tipping point when my choice became inevitable.

There is no doubt why unexpected and new events cause stress: It's a human response built into our DNA. Ambiguity is frightening, and it's natural to react with anxiety and worry when you consider leaving the comfort zone or when life thrusts you into the discomfort zone. But anxiety isn't an effective coping mechanism; it won't help you navigate your way through a crisis or into the confidence zone, where you will achieve your goals and create your best life. That's where the third step of the MOST model, stress tolerance, comes in.

Stress tolerance is the ability to cope with the challenges and obstacles that will arise during your journey out of the comfort zone. It enables you to manage them rather than allowing them to defeat you. In itself, stress is neither negative nor positive. It's our reaction to the stressor that determines the "good or bad" outcome. When we aren't used to moving beyond our comfort zone, we have very little ability to tolerate stress. Instead of stepping through the stressors and past them, with our coping skills as our shield, we hide and protect ourselves in the shelter of the comfort zone. Our old habits keep us safe, yet uninspired. Without coping skills to help us manage stress, uncertainty and ambiguity can send us into a tailspin. Our anxiety can spiral as we play out worst-case scenarios in our mind.

An optimistic mind-set will help you tolerate stress, but that's just the beginning. You need coping skills, too. Most people can handle a lot of pressure without losing productivity or effectiveness, but when a combination of stressors all hit at once, the MOST strategy becomes critical. Fortunately, emotional intelligence can help you understand your stress triggers so you can take preventative measures, building your stress tolerance skills so you're prepared when things go wrong.

The first step to improving your stress tolerance is to recognize when your reserves are low. Too often, we don't use our emotional intelligence to monitor our stress level. The pressure creeps up on us gradually. We often pile on the self-induced stress and then give ourselves little room for failure. I saw this recently when I met with a client who was getting ready to go on vacation with her husband.

Instead of seeing her trip as a chance to relax and take a break from stress, my friend put herself under an enormous amount of pressure. She worried about everything she needed to do at work and at home before she left. In the middle of venting her frustrations to me, she blurted out, "I've been so busy I haven't even had time to tell my husband what to do!" If my friend had recognized that she was putting unintentional stress on herself, she could have used her coping skills to calm down and actually look forward to her vacation.

Stress tolerance gives you the tools you need to take ambiguity in stride. When you're confident stepping out of your comfort zone, you're less anxious and more relaxed. You can think more clearly, have greater confidence when placing trust in others, and feel more capable of handling a variety of situations. An ability to handle stress lets you respond to events with mindfulness—to be present, read the situation, and make a good decision—because you're not overwhelmed by fear. Response is a choice. Resilience is the goal.

Comfort Zone Self-Reflection Exercise

1. How long has it been since you took a big risk?

   a. More than three years ago or never

   b. Between one year and three years ago

   c. Within the last twelve months

2. When was the last time you did something that embarrassed you?

   a. More than three years ago or never

   b. Between one year and three years ago

   c. Within the last twelve months

3. Thinking back over the last four weeks, how many of the activities you participated in gave you a sense of accomplishment?

   a. Less than 25 percent of them or none
   b. Some of them
   c. More than 50 percent of them

4. How long has it been since you tried something completely new?

   a. More than three years ago or never
   b. Between one year and three years ago
   c. Within the last twelve months

5. If you work, how long has it been since you changed jobs or changed roles in your current company?

   a. More than three years ago or never
   b. Between one year and three years ago
   c. Within the last twelve months

6. How often do you feel happy?

   a. Not often or never
   b. Sometimes
   c. The majority of the time

7. When was the last time you said no to something you wanted to do because you were afraid you would not succeed?

   a. Within the last twelve months
   b. Between one year and three years ago
   c. More than three years ago or never

8. How often do you catch yourself drifting or coasting through the day without a lot of presence of mind?

   a. The majority of the time
   b. Sometimes
   c. Not often or never

9. In the last four weeks, how many of the activities you participated in challenged you mentally or physically?

   a. Less than 25 percent of them or none
   b. Some of them
   c. More than 50 percent of them

10. When was the last time you were caught off guard or unprepared for a change in your life?

    a. Within the last twelve months
    b. Between one year and three years ago
    c. More than three years ago or never

Scoring Guide

For Questions Answered	Behavioral Tendencies	Growth Opportunities
A	You are likely drifting between the disengagement and comfort zones.	Time to shake things up! Look for opportunities to try new things and get uncomfortable.
B	You are likely living in your comfort zone and avoiding things that challenge or discourage you.	Push yourself into the discomfort zone more, take more risk, and see what you are capable of.
C	You likely have been pushing yourself into the discomfort and confidence zones on a regular basis. Congratulations!	Keep it up, and remember to maintain your motivation, optimism, and stress tolerance to sustain your positive growth.

In Summary—Build Your EQ Before a Crisis Hits

When you begin to practice the MOST strategies, you may be surprised to find how many facets of your life are affected. In large part, I have dedicated my career to helping people build their EQ because I have seen a universal benefit to people's whole life when they focus on developing those skills. When I help business clients learn to read their audience better, to manage their impulses, and to calibrate their responses to fit the people they're working with, they automatically start using those skills in their personal life, too.

I often hear from clients that the EQ skills they learned with me at work saved their marriage. Once, after I had given a keynote address, a woman approached me to say, "I need to thank you. My husband and I have been having a really hard time. I tend to be very direct and straightforward, and I've always told him, 'Look, this is who I am. If you can't accept that, you're the one with the problem.' But you've helped me to realize how unfair that is. I can adapt my behavior for him instead of just clinging to what's comfortable for me."

When my kids were young, not long after those dark days, Steve and I found ourselves with another big choice to make once Annie's health had stabilized and our immediate financial needs were met. We took a hard look at whether we should relocate from expensive, busy Southern California to a quieter, less-expensive lifestyle in New Hampshire. The lower cost of living and simpler way of life would ease the financial pressure on us, and we believed it would also help us avoid getting into similar problems again in the future.

Naturally, my comfort zone was solidly in Orange County: It's where I grew up, and my social and family network was there. The idea of leaving all of that to go somewhere I had no ties was *very* uncomfortable. But when I looked at the move through an optimistic lens, I could see that a fresh start in a new community could strengthen my marriage, because it would require us to rely on each other more. Our new town also offered a great public school system for my daughters, in a place without so much emphasis on looks, social status, and possessions.

Once I tapped into my motivation, I saw that New England would be a brand-new market for my business and services, which could lead to new and exciting projects. And, ultimately, I maintained my stress tolerance by planning the move almost a year ahead of time, making several visits to our new town before we finally loaded up the moving van. That gradual approach allowed me to slowly familiarize myself with the new surroundings, so I wasn't overwhelmed by having to figure out day care, learn my way around town without getting lost, and find my new grocery store all at once. We also made the decision to move in June so the kids could have the summer to meet the neighbors and adjust before jumping into a new school system.

Throughout the transition time, I hovered between my comfort and discomfort zones. But I kept my focus on my goal—the confidence zone—picturing myself in a beautiful new home with breathtaking surroundings, watching my daughters thrive in a wholesome community and getting a fresh start to my marriage. Eventually, I got there.

Funny enough, when we first arrived in our new town, Steve was still a stay-at-home dad, and I had taken a month off my travel to assist in the transition. Every time we met new neighbors, they asked if we had moved to New Hampshire because of a job relocation. We said, "No." They asked if we had moved to be closer to family. We said, "No, in fact we left family." We could see the curious look on their faces when we told them we had moved to New Hampshire from Southern California, since most people who relocate by choice move in the opposite direction—to warmer weather. After almost a month had gone by with neither Steve nor I heading off to a job every day, I am sure the neighbors were convinced we were in the witness protection program!

Just as Steve and I learned with our move to New England, the decisions you make may not always make sense to the people around you, even those who love and understand you best. It's important to trust yourself to know what's right for you and when it's time to make a change, rather than letting yourself be swayed by others' judgments and expectations. Have confidence that you are your own best guide as you consciously create your life and risk stepping into the discomfort zone. When you utilize the MOST model, you choose resilience.

It's also important to remember that a transition strategy doesn't form on its own. Sometimes you have to make some difficult short-term choices to benefit you in the long run, which requires conscious awareness and effort. I'm not telling you to take a leap of faith or even make a big cross-country move . . . I'm encouraging you to take a step toward progress in your own life. When you're ready to make your exit from the comfort zone, you can use the

CHAPTER 4

Motivation:
Lighting Your Internal Fire

I have met many people who are highly motivated, and I'm willing to bet that all of them would say they regularly push the boundaries of their own comfort zone. Having a strong drive—in other words, motivation—to achieve a specific outcome is one of the best ways to launch yourself out of your safe bubble. Are you ready to push beyond the comfort zone? Are you feeling inspired by what you learned about yourself when you completed the Comfort Zone Self-Reflection Exercise in Chapter 3?

Some people draw their motivation from doing work they are

passionate about. Others are striving toward a particular goal and get an energy boost each time they hit another milestone (like training for their first half-marathon and getting a thrill out of watching their run times improve). Some people feel they have a sense of control over their life and the confidence that they're strong enough to handle whatever is thrown at them; others (plenty of us) don't. If you aren't as happy as you'd like to be, or if you feel you need a confidence zone tune-up, the pages that follow may inspire you to take the next steps of your journey.

Just like I have met many go-getters, I also know plenty of people who are sleepwalking through life, not realizing that they would be so much happier if they made a life change. Others complain that they are not happy at work, with their partner, or with their physical health but seem unwilling to set a clear goal for improvement. Complaints and negativity beget more complaints and negativity. Goals, in contrast, create an opening for real change.

With a goal in mind, you're ready for an exit strategy: a plan for getting out of your comfort zone and moving toward joy, engagement, and fulfillment. In this chapter, we'll take a closer look at the importance of motivation for achieving your goals, and how to leverage it in order to find success beyond the limits of your comfort zone.

The Spark to Move

Your exit strategy begins with *motivation*—that's the fuel you need to get yourself up and moving. The comfort zone usually involves some degree of stagnation or stasis, and getting out of it is going to require you to act! Motivation is the buzz of internal energy that will drive you toward action.

If you've set a goal for yourself—to spend more quality time with your kids, to change to a more fulfilling career, or to get more healthy and fit—you know what your desire is. Motivation is the energy flow that will help you convert that desire into tangible change. Have you ever found yourself complaining about the same thing over and over again, or setting the same New Year's resolution a few years in a row? You say you want to change something, and you do—that's the desire piece—but you lack the energy to propel yourself into motion. You're not doing anything to advance toward your goal; you're lounging or even languishing in the comfort zone. That's where motivation comes in. Once you add energy to your desire for change, you have the motivation to take the necessary action to improve your situation.

I find that one of the best ways to cultivate that energy is to better understand *why* you desire a particular change. Below are some of the common reasons why people are willing to put forth effort to get out of the comfort zone and work toward achieving their goals. Which of these resonate for you? Maybe you have some of your own reasons that aren't included on this list.

One person wants to lose weight so he will to be alive to see his grandchildren; another wants to lose weight to feel good again after her marriage ends. One person chooses to work overtime because he wants to be able to send his teenager to college; another finds the motivation to work overtime to save for an early retirement.

The **Whys:** *Eight Common Motivators*

1. **Recognition:** You are energized by public acknowledgement and by being praised and valued for the things you do.

2. **Challenge:** You get a "high" from fixing things that others can't, and you specialize in creative solutions for difficult situations.

3. **Opportunity for growth:** You feel most alive when you are learning, so you take opportunities to develop yourself by enrolling in classes and trying out new skills and hobbies.

4. **Career advancement:** You derive satisfaction from building your responsibilities at work and progressing up the organizational chart, setting yourself on a path to career success.

5. **Money:** You feel jazzed about working hard to earn bonuses, commissions, or financial rewards because you see these as a sign of success and an opportunity to access more of the life you want.

6. **Making a difference:** You experience a sense of peace, happiness, and meaning when you work to improve the lives of others and make a contribution to society.

7. **Incentives:** You love the thrill of competitive activities and enjoy earning the prizes associated with

success (first place in a contest, a special recognition, a chance to travel).

8. **Work–life balance:** You have more energy for participating or leading when you have flexibility in your schedule and balance among the different areas of your life, such as work, family, and personal time.

Whichever reasons motivate you to step out of your own personal comfort zone, your "why" can be the spark that causes you to move.

Procrastination strikes all of us, and the more challenging or uncomfortable something is, the more likely we are to put it off until tomorrow. Yet there is always another tomorrow, and without a clear incentive, we may be likely to delay in perpetuity. Motivation helps us stay productive, even when our efforts are not all that enjoyable in the moment.

Ditching the Disengagement Blues

The opposite of motivation is disengagement: those times when you find yourself coasting through activities without much attention or enjoyment. At one time or another, you're bound to feel disengaged. It's unavoidable—not everything in life is fun. A recent Gallup poll found that 70 percent of Americans are disengaged at work.[1] That's pretty disheartening at first glance. But it's important to remember that engagement is a spectrum that we slide back and forth on throughout the course of a year. The whole country isn't moving through life on autopilot. Rather, we're all at different points on a wheel, cycling from engagement to disengagement and back again, in all the facets of our lives.

Disengagement often starts out as a diminishing interest or an unwillingness to put in extra effort. You might show up to work but drift through the workday, watch the clock, and do the minimum. Once in a while, we all have days like that. The key is to regularly self-monitor, so that you recognize when you're "phoning it in" more often than you're engaged in what you're doing.

I am honestly surprised—not by how many people are disengaged—but by how few people seem to be doing anything about it. I can't help asking myself, "Why would they want to live like that?" Choosing to stay in a job to which you don't feel any connection isn't good for anyone. Neither is shuffling through your daily routine without any true sense of enjoyment. We can point fingers at our employers for creating a negative work environment, or we can blame the frantic pace of modern life, but when we start to employ more EQ, we take responsibility for our own happiness instead of accepting the circumstances we find ourselves in.

Not only can it be a challenge to stay motivated at work, we can find our energy waning at home, too. Activities that were once easy or enjoyable start to feel mundane or like drudgery. When my children were young, my nightly ritual of making dinner, washing the dishes, bathing the kids, singing lullabies or reading books, and getting them into bed started to feel so tedious, I found myself dreading the dinner hour as it approached. Did we really have to go through that whole process every night? I was grumpy, and it showed—so naturally, my kids were grumpy, too. I was itching to get out of my repetitive at-home comfort zone, while still being a good mom and staying engaged with my kids.

After a few months of this nightly slog, I put my EQ to work. When I spent some time reflecting on what I was actually feeling and why, I *recognized* that I was bored, plain and simple. I loved my kids, and being a fun and engaged mom was very important to me, but I was so sick of that darn routine that had to be completed every evening. I'm someone who likes challenge and variety, and I just wasn't getting it from my evenings with the girls.

Once I understood the problem (my boredom) and what was causing it (lack of variety), I took a fresh look at my motivation (to be a great mom). Was I being a great mom during that boring nightly routine? What impact was my attitude having on my children? Were they really getting the best from me?

Clearly, they weren't. People tend to mirror your emotions, and the girls had picked up on mine. They were acting up at bedtime, not cooperating, popping out of bed for just a little more attention. I really wasn't being a great mom in that moment. Since that's a powerful motivation for me, it was well worth it to me to put in the effort to overcome the problem.

Once I had that clarity, I could formulate a goal: Be fun and present with my daughters while finding more enjoyment in the nighttime routine. From there, it was a matter of *reading* for opportunities to inject fun into the process or mix things up a bit, then *responding* by seizing those opportunities, making changes that would suit all of us in that particular moment.

Some nights, this meant that instead of cooking dinner, I played a board game with the girls and ordered a pizza. Some nights, I gave them their baths *before* dinner, so we had time to be silly and goof around a little bit without the pressure of bedtime. There were nights the dishes stayed in the sink until the next morning. Of course, there were also nights when I didn't have the patience to deal with the kids, so I sent them upstairs to brush their teeth while I did the dishes in peace and quiet. I used my emotional intelligence to monitor my emotional needs. This helped keep me motivated in the short term and engaged over the long term. My constant goal was (and is) to be a great mom, and that helped me get over the hump of the discomfort zone and into the confidence zone.

Changing Motivations Over Time

It helps to remember that our driving forces change as we mature, so the things that incentivized you when you were younger might have lost their effectiveness over the years. You might just be going through the motions, disengaged without even realizing it.

This was the situation that recently challenged my friend Anna. When her daughter was young, Anna had volunteered to lead a Girl Scout troop. It was a little outside her comfort zone at the time—she wasn't a natural leader and wasn't sure she was up to the task. However, it was a chance to spend time with her daughter, doing something they both enjoyed, and Anna felt like she needed more challenge in her life.

Four years later, Anna was still leading the Girl Scout troop. But her life looked a lot different than it had when her daughter was in kindergarten. Over the years, Anna had increased her working hours and taken on bigger, more interesting projects. She'd also started writing a novel—an adventure she never dreamed she'd undertake, but inspired her to spend every spare minute typing away on her laptop. She'd begun to resent the hours she spent planning for Girl Scout meetings, the emails and organizational duties, even the time spent on field trips and outings. She'd become disengaged.

When Anna and I talked it over, she realized that she'd lost the motivation she'd started out with. What had once been an interesting challenge had become a chore. She found fulfillment in working toward other goals now. The time she devoted to the troop was actually pulling her away from those goals. As we talked, it dawned on her that her only motivation for being a Scout leader was to make sure she didn't disappoint her daughter. That didn't feel like enough anymore. Anna asked another parent to take on some of the responsibilities of leadership, which gave her more time to pursue her new goals without letting her daughter down.

There are a number of reasons why people like Anna become disengaged:

- Boredom that comes from routine, mundane, or repetitive activities.
- Overwork that leads to burnout. Maybe you have been in the same job or volunteer role too long and lost interest. Or maybe the position was a bad fit for you all along, and you are finally realizing or admitting it.
- A significant life change (a return to school, a new job or promotion, a new baby, illness, etc.) that demands your energy and all your effort, causing you to pull back from other obligations that feel less important.

- A perceived professional trauma of some sort, such as being passed over for a promotion, feeling unappreciated, or being unhappy with your compensation. Similarly, some people disengage as a passive–aggressive reaction to an over-controlling boss.
- A passive approach to your career or life path, so that you are rolling with whatever happens to you instead of deciding what you want and working toward it.

Ways to get motivated and reengage include the following:

- Identify the activities that bring you the most satisfaction, and incorporate more of them into your life, interspersed among the mundane tasks, as a way to reenergize yourself.
- Mix up the order in which you accomplish tasks, or take a different route to work.
- Make a list of the benefits you experience when you put in some extra effort (what will you get from it?), and post it on the wall or keep it in your wallet.
- Ask for a different role at work or a different set of responsibilities.
- Acknowledge that you may be feeling unmotivated, and identify the root cause.

Another helpful approach is taking a motivation inventory every few years. Sit down with a piece of paper and list all the goals you're working toward and all the commitments you're spending your energy on. Then go back through the list and fill in the *why*: What's driving you toward that goal? Are you still invested in that project? Are you making progress on a regular basis? This is the time to gauge whether there's still a match between your motivation and the goals you're working toward. Maybe you have been avoiding the uninteresting and challenging activities, thinking that would make you happy, but instead it's left you feeling unfulfilled. We each have a unique passcode that unlocks our inspiration, our potential, and our desire to achieve.

It's Never Too Late

A common challenge to staying motivated is that little voice inside your head that tells you, "It's too late for me to start working toward this goal, so why bother?" Some people would say it's too late to buy your first house in your forties, or change careers in your fifties, or finish that degree in your sixties, but I don't think so. In many ways, pursuing and achieving goals keeps you young. I recently spoke with a woman who was lamenting that if she went back to school, she wouldn't finish her degree until she was fifty. I said, "Well, you're going to be fifty anyway. Why not have a diploma to go with it?"

Another key to maintaining motivation is keeping in mind that nothing lasts forever. The world is a dynamic place, and even the most difficult circumstances and the problems that really test us pass eventually. If you can remember that the crisis isn't permanent, you may find yourself more motivated to power through.

I've learned this lesson through tough experience. My business took a real hit in the economic downturn of 2008–2009. As a result, I found myself in a big financial mess, running a negative cash flow each month. The situation was unsustainable. I only had one employee at the time, but it was becoming impossible to make her payroll plus mine. I had taken all the pay cuts I could afford and was running into another personal financial crisis.

Finally, I knew I had a huge choice to make: deny the situation I was in and postpone taking any action, or do something that was incredibly uncomfortable and painful and lay off my employee. She had worked for me for four years and had been an excellent employee, so I felt just awful. I put it off for a while, dreading the conversation and not wanting to admit my failure to myself, my employee, and the clients I would also have to tell. And have I mentioned that she was nine months pregnant?

I flew to Denver to see her in person, since she was a remote worker. I had an upset stomach the entire flight. She met me at the airport with her husband and two-year-old son. I considered waiting until the end of her maternity leave to tell her I couldn't bring her back full time, but I knew that delaying the inevitable to alleviate my discomfort would have deprived her of valuable time to find another job. So I bit the bullet and said what I had to say. It was painful and very difficult.

While she was on leave, I doubled down on my efforts to build up my business. Pride drove me to find ways to recover. By the time her maternity leave ended a few months later, I had been able to pick up a small project and could use some part time help, so I called her. She hadn't found another job and was happy for the work. I ended up using her on a part-time basis for another year, and she managed to scrape by on half a salary. Eventually my business rebounded, and she came back to work for me full time.

That day at the airport, I was so dejected and felt so unmotivated.

It felt like everything I had worked for was falling apart. But my love for the business I had built and my sense of responsibility to my employee and clients served as powerful motivators, and with hard work and determination, I was able to turn the business around. I have taken that experience with me and always remember that good times do return.

Feeling Unmotivated? Tap Into the Power of EQ

When you're struggling with a similar challenge, it's easy to become drained and discouraged. If the stress goes on too long, your fatigue might grow into exhaustion and a sense of powerlessness. Feeling lost can be paralyzing. You might not know what else to do, so you do nothing. You shut down.

You might also feel this way if you're suffering from a *lack* of challenge. Many of us have felt this way about our work life at one time or another. It's not uncommon for people to end up in their career by default instead of by design. Maybe they stayed with that first job they happened to land out of school, or maybe they joined the family business. At some point, we might find ourselves in a job that we can do competently, but that doesn't provide us any real satisfaction or meaning. The days start to feel long and exhausting. We have the sense that we are *giving* so much more than we are *getting*.

Whichever situation you're in, the cure is the same: motivation. Keeping yourself motivated is the key to breaking into a more productive zone and staying on the leading edge of the challenges you face.

You don't want to wait to make a change until you are in a crisis. It can be easy to delay working toward change when there's no sense of urgency, but a focus on motivation propels you beyond the status quo and in the direction of your goals before an emergency forces your hand. Once you jump in, you'll probably find that it wasn't as difficult as you imagined.

But how can you stay motivated? What if you don't know what truly motivates you? That's where your emotional intelligence comes in. You can use the three *R*s (recognize, read, respond) to determine what motivates you, formulate a goal, and then seek out opportunities to move yourself forward.

Recognize

The first step in the process of motivation is to check in with yourself and take the measure of where you are right now in relation to your comfort zone. How long has it been since you challenged yourself? What have you been avoiding because it makes you uncomfortable? Recognize whether you've been feeling disengaged or unfulfilled, and then begin to reflect on why. Resist the urge to assign reasons to others or outside factors.

For example, instead of saying, "I wish I had a better social life, but I'm stuck living in this small town because that's where my job is," ask yourself, "Why is my social life unfulfilling?" If the answer is that you haven't met many people, then why is that the case? If it's because you're working long hours, then why are you working so much? Keep pushing until you get to the root cause of the problem. When you can recognize what the real issue is, your motivation to change will be clearer, and you'll be able to formulate an exit strategy.

You probably picked up this book because you were interested in stretching the limits of your comfort zone. As you read the first few chapters, you might have recognized an aspect of your own life that you wanted to change, and if you've been following my prompts for deeper reflection, you've probably formulated a goal to work toward. You're beginning to achieve a new level of self-awareness.

Read

Once you've recognized the need for change, you can look for ways to make that change happen. That's the *read* piece of the motivation puzzle: to read your environment for opportunities for change and growth. It's okay to start small, just doing one thing every day that makes you uncomfortable. The key is to scan for chances to push your own boundaries. Did your self-reflection reveal that you want to live with more authenticity? When you catch yourself pushing your emotions aside to avoid a confrontation, there's your opportunity. Did you realize that you need to let go of some control over your household? When your teenager offers to make dinner (even though you know it'll barely be edible), there's your opportunity.

Respond

Then, once you've read your environment for opportunities, *respond* to them. Make that leap. Take advantage of the chance you identified to push out of your comfort zone and move toward your goal. It might be uncomfortable. It might be intense, and you might not succeed. But your motivation will help you pick yourself up off the ground, recalibrate, and try again.

Let's take a look at some examples of how we might apply the three *R*s to the motivation process:

The Role the Three Rs Play in Motivation

Goal	Recognize (the "Why")	Read (the "What")	Respond (the "How")
To move out of your customer service job and into sales	Recognize that you've become bored with your work and you want the challenge and variety of a job in sales.	Observe that a coworker in the sales department is struggling under a heavy client load.	Talk to your boss about your goal, and ask if you might begin a transition into sales by helping your coworker with his or her workload.
To become more financially stable	Recognize that living beyond your means is causing you unnecessary anxiety.	Review your budget for luxuries you can do without.	Have a portion of your paycheck automatically deposited into your savings account.
To improve your relationship with your spouse	Recognize that you've fallen into a pattern of negative thinking and criticism.	Look for situations when you can offer warmth and gratitude.	Act on those situations by speaking up with kindness.

In Summary—Embrace Change on Your Own Terms

Exiting your comfort zone requires an awakening. It's easy to be lulled into a false sense of security, mistaking comfort for contentment or stability for happiness. While it's important to have food, shelter, income, and all the basics for survival, don't confuse surviving with thriving—the next level of fulfillment, where we are feeding not just our body but our mind and our spirit—our whole person.

When you realize the importance of proactively taking action, you'll begin to test your limits and redefine your capacity for growth. You'll probably find that you're energized by this new, dynamic approach to your life. That energy and drive toward positive change can revive your reputation at work and take you well beyond the mundane safety net of an unfulfilling job. It can revitalize your marriage, inspire you to get your MBA, or get you off the couch and into the gym.

The fact is, we have the capacity to embrace new habits long before a crisis forces us to do so. I am sure you can reflect back on a chapter in your life when you were given no alternative but to take action because circumstances pushed you out of the nest and forced you to take flight before you felt ready.

Unfortunately, we don't always have the benefit of a gentle nudge encouraging us to venture outside our zone of comfort. The push often comes like a two-by-four across the head, with the shocking realization that change is happening, whether we like it or not. It may take the form of a layoff, a demotion, or a bad performance review. Maybe it's your doctor telling you that those extra twenty pounds you've been planning to lose have earned you a sky-high cholesterol level. Whatever your particular catalyst is, if you've been forced into urgent change, you know it's no fun.

When we learn to use our EQ for a deeper self-awareness, we can recognize the need for change before it's imposed on us. We can respond in the way that fits us best, because we have the luxury of transitioning on our own terms and at our own pace.

Endnote

1 Amy Adkins, "Majority of U.S. Employees Not Engaged Despite Gains in 2014," Gallup, January 28, 2015, http://www.gallup.com/poll/181289/majority-employees-not-engaged-despite-gains-2014.aspx.

CHAPTER 5

Optimism: Seeing the Light Beyond the Darkness

W e've talked about the importance of motivation for moving out of your comfort zone and achieving your goals, but motivation isn't enough unless you also have optimism. The two are natural partners: Motivation helps you recognize what you want to achieve and gives you the drive to get there, while optimism gives you the confidence that you can overcome any obstacles standing between you and what you want to accomplish. I may be motivated to get on my elliptical in the morning, but it's my optimism about the results I'll achieve that keeps me going when I've hit the thirty-minute mark and my body's starting to hurt, I've got a stitch in my side, and I just want to quit.

Just like motivation is critical to our ability to persevere when things get scary outside our comfort zone, we must also maintain a positive attitude and know that things will get better and easier on the other side. Optimism will serve us well in any situation, but it becomes critical when we're facing a significant hardship or taking a big leap into the confidence zone.

Optimism is the belief that you can and will achieve your goals. It is a positive and realistic mind-set that understands that challenges will arise during your journey through the four quadrants, as well as the confidence to know you can work through these challenges with determination and creativity.

Optimism as it's defined in the MOST model isn't just a decision to look on the bright side. It's much more complex than that. True optimism involves reading a situation honestly and accepting circumstances as they are, instead of wishing they were different or dwelling on the negative. It's about recognizing negative thought patterns in yourself and in others and responding in ways that replace those patterns with healthier, more positive thinking.

Negative thought patterns create pessimism, the enemy of optimism. Have you ever shared a great idea or an exciting plan with others, only to have them rain on your parade with pessimistic comments and questions that suggest you won't be able to accomplish your goals? "That sounds expensive." "Won't that take a long time?" "Sounds like you have an uphill battle on that one." Fill in the blank . . . we've all heard this kind of negative statement before. Don't give in to the pessimism of others or of your inner critic. Optimism lines the pathway to the confidence zone!

Optimism will help you see challenges as opportunities and potential roadblocks as stepping stones—not because you are Pollyanna or naïve but because you trust your own ability to come up with novel solutions and outside-the-bubble approaches, and you believe you'll be met with support when you reach out to others. In short, an optimistic mind-set keeps your ideas and energy flowing.

As I share my thoughts on optimism with you in this chapter, I don't intend in any way to minimize any struggle or difficulty you might be experiencing. Instead, I want to remind you of your own innate ability to instigate positive change and the resilience you have for overcoming current and future hardships. The problems you're facing may not be small, and the goals you've set for yourself may sometimes feel hard to achieve, but when you're confident in your own strength and sure of your ability to handle whatever life throws at you, you *will* rise to the challenge.

The key to being more resilient is to reach inside yourself and bring to the surface all the untapped resources you possess: your courage, your capacity for innovative and creative problem solving, and your ability to adapt to change.

Finding My Optimism in the Darkness

In the weeks after my daughter Annie was born, when we were struggling with her diagnosis and the appropriate treatment, I had a powerful motivation: to resolve the problems with her kidney and get her as healthy as she could possibly be. It was much harder for me to manage optimism. It was difficult to believe that everything would be okay and that I possessed the skills needed to help steer us there. It took a while before I had any sense of control over the circumstances we found ourselves in.

When Annie was just twelve weeks old, the doctors recommended that the best treatment for her was to remove her nonfunctional kidney, to eliminate the risk of problems down the road. The surgeon we met with wanted to do the operation immediately, saying it was risky to wait. But Annie was so tiny, still a newborn, and the idea of sending her into surgery terrified me. I also knew that the operation would leave my little girl with a long scar that ran across her belly. I hated the idea of that, but I had no prior experience with serious health problems, so who was I to say? I was blessed to come from a healthy family who had never had to make such tough decisions.

My first instinct was to listen to the doctor: He was the expert, and he certainly knew more than I did about the best course of action. I also secretly liked the finality of putting the situation behind us. With Annie's kidney removed, we'd never have to deal with the problem again. My pediatrician concurred, so we scheduled her surgery. I insisted that it be done at our local children's hospital and was assured that it would be.

A week before the surgery, I received a call from the doctor's office saying that we had a problem. Unbeknownst to us, our surgeon did not have privileges at the children's hospital. He had arranged for an assisting doctor (who did have access) to be in attendance, but the office was calling to advise us that the second doctor had a conflict and could not be there for Annie's surgery. As a result, they wanted to move Annie's surgery to the general hospital. This was very upsetting news to me. I wanted my newborn in a hospital that catered to her needs, but waiting for the assisting surgeon to be available meant delaying this critical surgery by several months. Although the doctor's office was pressuring me to agree to the change in hospital, I requested twenty-four hours to make my final decision.

I woke up discouraged the next morning. Steve and I considered giving in and changing hospitals, and then I tapped into my optimism. Couldn't we still get what we wanted for Annie in the time frame we needed? Yes! It hit me that we had not gotten a second opinion. What had we been thinking? I immediately got online and found a pediatric nephrology center within thirty miles of our home. Why hadn't my pediatrician mentioned this as an option? I called the center as soon as it opened and explained my problem. They said, "Come in and we will see you today."

We ended up meeting with a talented young doctor who looked over Annie's condition and determined that she did not need a kidney removal—he could perform a simple outpatient procedure to drain the blockage. He advised that there was still a 90 percent chance that Annie would need a bigger surgery later, but he also said that the alternative treatment would buy us enough time that if she did need her kidney removed, she would be old enough that it could be done via laparoscopic surgery, without leaving any scars. We were thrilled and changed surgeons immediately.

It turned out that the new doctor did such an amazing job that, fifteen years later, Annie has not needed any additional surgeries. Sometimes I ask myself, "What if I hadn't insisted on getting that second opinion?" If I hadn't stepped in and taken back some control over this situation instead of feeling completely powerless, my little baby would have had an unnecessary and very invasive surgery.

When it seems you have hit a roadblock, instead of automatically giving in to the negative, ask yourself, "Is it possible to get the outcome I want? What can I do to make that happen?" Almost everything is possible. Instead of yes–no or black-and-white thinking, consider the gray in between. Ask yourself, is there a third way? The solution may not come via the path you originally planned on, but by using a little creative thinking, you can usually find ways to make it happen. That's the power of optimism—rationality and creativity working in tandem.

Are You an Optimist or a Pessimist?

Optimism doesn't just help propel you toward your goals. Significant research has shown that optimism has a lasting impact on people's happiness and resiliency. Martin Seligman is the leading researcher on the topic of optimism and positive psychology; he runs the Authentic Happiness Institute at the University of Pennsylvania. In his book *Learned Optimism,* Seligman wrote that "the defining characteristic of pessimists is that they tend to believe that bad events will last a long time, will undermine everything they do. . . . The optimists, who are confronted with the same hard knocks of this world, think about misfortune in the opposite way. They tend to believe that defeat is just a temporary setback or a challenge, that its causes are just confined to this one case."[1]

When faced with misfortune, pessimists commonly look outward in their search for the cause. Instead of owning their part in the problem and taking steps toward fixing it, they find someone or something else to blame. But that leads to a sense of no control and hopelessness, which keeps them stuck in the comfort zone. They don't seem to realize that if they could identify their role in their circumstances, they'd pinpoint how they could change their situation for the better. Instead of leveraging their personal power, they waste loads of time and energy complaining about their issues. "Bad luck" lets them off the hook for taking action and personal responsibility.

Even if you generally take ownership of your actions, pessimism can still creep in, a little voice in your head that disguises itself as the truth. All of us listen to that voice sometimes. Consider the following examples of optimism versus pessimism. Which attitude seems more familiar to you?

Do you typically expect a negative outcome and react accordingly?

- "I'll never be able to lose all this weight before my sister's wedding—why bother trying?"
- "I shouldn't even think about applying for that job. I don't have enough experience, and they'll never hire me."
- "If I try to talk to my friend about how she's been relying too much on me, she'll get offended, and we'll have a fight. I had better just keep my mouth shut."

Or do you take a realistic look at your goals and figure out how to achieve them?

- "Even if I don't hit my weight goal before my sister's wedding, all that healthy eating and exercise will have me feeling great about how I look."
- "I know this job is a stretch, but I'm going to do everything I can to present myself as a desirable candidate. If they don't hire me, I'll keep on working and looking till I get a job that I really love."
- "I'm nervous to have this talk with my friend, but everything is going to work out okay. Hopefully she will understand what I'm saying; if not, I will be proud of myself for setting boundaries and taking care of my needs."

Which of these thought patterns—if you're really honest with yourself—is more familiar to you? Take some time to think about which of the statements above have the power to move you, and which have the power to keep you from moving forward. Did you feel energized by the optimistic statements? Did you feel stagnant and despondent when you read the pessimistic thoughts? Without realizing it, you might have been letting a pessimistic attitude undermine your courage to start moving into the confidence zone. Has that little voice kept you fearful of taking risks and trying something new? Optimism and pessimism are both powerful, but only one of them moves you out of the comfort zone.

You might not be able to silence that pessimistic voice in your head for good, but you can find ways to disarm and reframe it. It can be helpful to borrow some techniques from the playbook of cognitive–behavioral therapy, which teaches people to identify cognitive distortions and refute them. When you catch yourself in the act of a negative thought pattern, take a moment to carefully examine that thought and reframe it. Maybe you're overgeneralizing one negative event and assuming it will keep on happening ("My ex-husband had an affair, so I'm never going to trust another man. They all cheat when given the chance."). Maybe you're catastroph-izing ("My boss didn't like that report I submitted. I'm going to get fired, and I'll never be able to find another job, and we'll have to sell our house and move in with my mom."). If you learn to stop these negative thought patterns in their tracks and replace them with healthier thinking, over time they'll eventually fade away. It is important to stay grounded in the facts of a situation without allowing yourself to get swept up in the drama.

Five Ways to Be More Optimistic

1. **Be mindful of your first reaction to assume the worst.** Ask yourself, "What about this situation could work out well?"

2. **Catch yourself (or ask a trusted friend or colleague to catch you) when you use negative language.** Phrases such as "Fat chance," "Don't waste your breath," "I have the worst luck," and "Nothing will change" all reveal your pessimistic expectations about the situation.

3. **Find your happy place.** Visualize yourself in the future living your best life, with your goals accomplished and your stressors removed, surrounded by the people who bring out the best in you.

4. **Don't believe everything you think.** Challenge yourself to change your thinking, and you will change your behavior. Interview yourself when you anticipate the worst to happen. Ask yourself, "Why do I have such low expectations of this situation? What are the odds that the worst-case scenario will actually happen? Are there actions I can take to mitigate any risk? What if the best outcome happened?"

5. **Lose the pessimists in your life.** Free yourself of relationships that bring out the worst in you, and make a date with an optimist. Good feelings and positive attitudes are contagious (just like the negative ones). Work to surround yourself in your business and personal life with people who make you feel strong, successful, valuable, energized, and happy.

Zoning in on Optimism

Probably the most important way to leverage your optimism is to use it to power you through the zones. If you have set a goal that requires some time and effort, you will need to head out of the disengagement or comfort zone and into the confidence zone.

The only way to that destination is through the dreaded discomfort zone—fueled by a healthy dose of optimism. When you keep the potential for positive outcomes in mind, it will help you fight through the discomfort zone (where you tackle the things that might not be pleasant but are productive).

Cycling Through the Four Quadrants

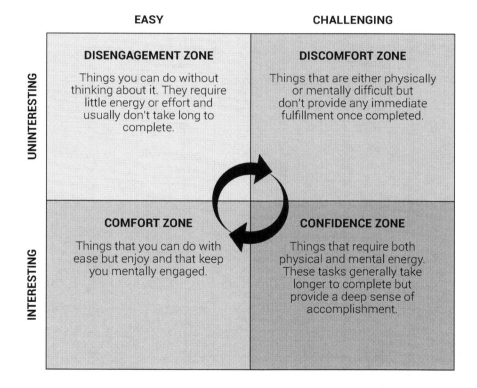

I have met people who recognize that they are in the disengagement or comfort zone and talk to me about the ways they wish their life were different. When I make a suggestion about things they could try, I hear, "Yeah, but." We've probably all fallen into the "yeah, but" trap ourselves from time to time. But people who are able to embrace optimism stop making excuses. They don't allow fear to be the endgame that stops them from toughing it out in the discomfort zone. Optimism helps us see that even if we don't succeed the way we hoped, we still will have learned something important in the process, and the effort is not wasted. Stepping out of the comfort zone always pays off, often in ways we don't expect.

It's also important to remember that your journey through the quadrants might not always be a perfect circle. Imagine that you started a diet and exercise plan in October. In the beginning, you were highly committed to your goals, and you were starting to see success—you'd become more fit and lost ten pounds. You'd made it into the discomfort zone and were well on your way to the confidence zone. But then the holidays hit, and in all the bustle, you found it harder to make time to exercise, and you didn't stick to your diet with all that yummy holiday food tempting you. You might feel discouraged when you get on the scale, but remember, the path to success is rarely a straight line.

Instead of giving up the diet completely and dwelling on the fact that you gained back all the weight you had just worked so hard to lose, appreciate how much you enjoyed yourself at the holiday parties and mealtimes without worrying about your weight. And then begin anew on your journey toward achieving your goal instead of living with regret. Chances are that you will get back into the healthy exercise and eating routine more quickly the second time around, since it is becoming familiar to you. It's not unlike the research that shows it may take multiple tries to quit smoking.[2] Falling back after a first attempt to change a behavior can actually be part of the normal process of making change.

So remember, it's okay if you find yourself retreating back to the comfort zone for a while to regroup. Keeping your optimism high helps you remember that it's a temporary break, one that is well earned, instead of beating yourself up or demoralizing yourself to the point of quitting. Reminding yourself that you will reach your goals, no matter what, will ensure that your time in the comfort zone is a short stopover, not a permanent derailment.

Balancing Optimism With Reality

As I mentioned earlier, optimism is important, but it needs to be balanced with a healthy dose of EQ. Your emotional intelligence is a powerful tool that you can use to read interpersonal situations and assess the mood of the people around you before you jump in with a positive outlook. If your best friend just broke up with her boyfriend, she may be just fine on her own, knowing she'll eventually fall in love again—but she still needs a hug and some time to cry without being cheered up just yet.

I once worked with a senior sales leader who was a classic optimist. Bill always had a smile on his face and an upbeat demeanor. His customers loved working with him, and he made everyone around him feel better. His optimism had served him well in his career and in his personal life. But during the time I worked with him, he learned the importance of tempering his optimism with emotional intelligence.

One of the products Bill's team sold to customers was very popular but unprofitable, so the company decided to discontinue it. His team was very upset, knowing that their customers would be mad and that they had some tough conversations ahead of them. They were worried about what the loss of their most popular product would mean for their team: How much would commission be affected? Would they keep their jobs?

The day of the announcement, Bill called an emergency meeting to discuss the issue. He led the meeting with his usual upbeat attitude, minimizing the team's concerns and reminding them that everything would work out just fine. His blind positivity only served to annoy his team more. Later, one of Bill's salespeople told me that throughout the meeting, all she could think was, "How can you be smiling right now?" With more EQ, Bill would have understood that his employees were shocked and still absorbing the bad news. They weren't ready for him to put a positive spin on things yet.

When I debriefed with Bill later, he admitted that he has a hard time listening to people complain. "It's one of my pet peeves," he told me. "I can't stand sitting in a meeting listening to people grumble. It drives me crazy. Let's just accept the problem and move on to solving it."

Bill's optimism was one of his strengths. However, he needed to balance it better by using EQ. Bill should have read the mood of that meeting room and understood that his team needed to vent their anger and frustration and that he needed to set his optimism aside temporarily. He should have stepped outside his comfort zone of positivity to give his team a chance to air their concerns and feel that he was standing by them.

After that, his team likely would have been ready for his positivity.

He could have told them, "Okay, we've talked about our concerns and gotten them all off our chest. Now let's talk about how we're going to solve the problem." At that point, Bill's optimism would have been the strength that guided the whole team through the ordeal. Instead, his attitude only turned them off.

The other end of the spectrum, unchecked pessimism, can be just as damaging, if not more so. And, as we've already discussed, pessimism can spread like a virus. I recently took my daughters out to dinner at one of our favorite restaurants. The waitress was someone we'd never had before, and we could tell from the moment we sat down that she just did not want to be at work that day. She was unfriendly, a little impatient with us, and curt—clearly in a bad mood and not enjoying her job at all.

When people don't like their job, you can always tell. The problem is, it creates a cycle. She was unpleasant to us, so we had a negative experience and didn't give her a very good tip. That probably put her in an even worse mood, so her next customers likely didn't tip her well, either. If she had just put on a good attitude or even smiled at us and said, "Please bear with me, I'm having a really rotten day" (using a little EQ), we would have responded with a "We've all been there" attitude and likely would have given her a good tip, and her day would have improved. It's a small example, but then again, it's not. I have to wonder how the waitress's negative attitude affected her ability to create the life she desired.

Just like in Bill's case, a little bit of emotional intelligence would have gone a long way in this situation. If our waitress had stopped to check in with herself when she noticed her bad mood, she might have realized, "I'm miserable today, but it's not really about work, it's because I got in a fight with my boyfriend this morning." Instead, she let that negativity spill into her next interaction. Pessimism was her comfort zone, and she was firmly settled there, instead of bravely putting on a cheerful face and taking responsibility for her own mood.

These two examples fall at extreme ends of the spectrum, but there are plenty of times in everyone's life when just a little bit of optimism can make a huge difference. Consider these situations where an automatic, negative response can be softened with a dose of optimism.

When your wife complains that she has to walk the dog again:

- "Why am I the only one responsible for the family pet? I'm just as busy as you are!" versus
- "Thank you for taking time to take care of the dog while I've been so busy with work lately. I really appreciate it. I could use a walk myself; why don't we take care of it together tonight after dinner?"

When your boss assigns you yet another project on top of your already full workload:

- "How am I supposed to manage this? I'm working late every night as it is!" versus
- "I'm excited to take on this project, and there's a lot I can learn from it. My workload is pretty heavy right now, though. Can we meet to review the projects I'm working on and see whether any can be reassigned to a colleague?"

When your son's first-grade teacher calls to tell you that he has been disrupting the class yet again:

- "Look, I'm doing the best I can! Can't you keep him more engaged in the lessons?" versus
- "How can we work together to make sure he's motivated to behave and becomes more interested in learning?"

Again, these are small examples that could have a big impact on helping you drive out of the comfort zone and toward creating the life you desire in the confidence zone. Think how much easier it will be to stretch and achieve when you have not only a positive belief that you can succeed but also your loved ones, colleagues, and community supporting you because you've enlisted them through your optimism and positivity.

Attitude is contagious. There is an old saying that "one bad apple spoils the whole bunch"—in other words, one person with a bad attitude can influence others to start feeling and acting the same way. Science has proven that mirror neurons in our brain respond in sync with people around us, and the closer our emotional connection to other people is, the more we subconsciously respond in kind.[3] This is the *read* part of emotional intelligence: empathy. That means that not only does a pessimistic attitude hurt you, it can negatively influence everyone around you, including your spouse, children, coworkers, and friends.

Of course, the opposite is true as well: If you approach life with an optimistic attitude, you are likely to find that your loved ones are optimistic, too. When you surround yourself with people who are positive and believe in the possibility of change, you'll form a powerful team of people who can support each other and work together to achieve your goals.

See the table below for examples of how the three *R*s can serve as tools to increase your optimism.

Optimism and the Three Rs

Scenario	Recognize	Read	Respond
You've been sending out résumés for months and still haven't gotten an interview.	Check in with yourself, and recognize that you are starting to believe there's no point in even trying to look for another job.	Read the situation for a more realistic interpretation, and realize that you can make changes to your résumé and your job search to market yourself better.	Meet with people in your professional network for input, rework your résumé, and put a different focus on your job search.
You have a chronic illness that causes you daily pain and limits your ability to be active.	Reassess your outlook, and recognize that you have become depressed and given up hope of leading a full, active life.	Take a more accurate read of your situation, change the expectations you are putting on yourself, and find solutions that work within your current constraints.	Explore holistic methods of pain management, find ways to be as active as possible within your limits, and develop a new hobby or interest.
You're sick of having the same fight with your spouse, over and over again.	Take a deeper look at your thought patterns, and recognize that you've built up anger and resentment over this issue and it's damaging your marriage.	Read the situation more honestly to look for ways you have been playing into the negative dynamic.	Make an effort to change the way you respond to your spouse's behavior, and tell him or her that you know you are both at fault and you'd like to work together to improve the situation.

The Power of Gratitude

If you can't already tell, I am driven, focused, ambitious, goal oriented, and competitive. I have been described as a perfectionist. Sometimes I have a hard time stopping to celebrate success, because I am so focused on the future and what still needs to be done. My natural drive for constant improvement can tend toward negativity if I'm not careful—I'm always looking for the next thing that needs fixing.

Because I'm aware of this tendency, I use my EQ to constantly monitor my own emotional state. When I'm boarding a plane after a successful speaking engagement, I try not to open up my laptop right away to get a jump start on the next project. Instead, I take a moment to pull back and reflect on what I've just accomplished. If I just spent an hour and a half speaking to an audience of several thousand, and I kept them engaged and interested the whole time—well, that's something to be proud of, and I should take a minute to reflect on what I did well (instead of my instinctive reaction to start thinking about how to improve my talk for next time).

In today's world of social media brag posts and reality TV's "keeping up with" culture, it is easy to feel like what we have or accomplish is never enough. Everyone else seems to be taking better vacations, throwing their children more impressive birthday parties, advancing through their career faster, and looking better in their swimsuit in those beach pictures. It's easy to focus on what other people have that we don't—but that line of thinking only serves to drive up our credit card debt, to-do list, and stress levels and sends us into a spiral of self-doubt and anxiety.

One thing I have noticed about the happiest people—they are grateful. They don't dwell on the negative in their life; they accept what's happened, deal with it, and focus on their many blessings. I'm not suggesting that you need to be cheerful every moment of every day. We have all faced dark times when we've looked bleakly toward the future, wondering how to get beyond the present moment when the circumstances seemed to offer very little hope or encouragement.

I have certainly felt my fair share of despair. I never thought that I would be divorced from the father of my children or be away from my family traveling so much. The key is not to come to a standstill and dwell on the negatives in our life. It takes courage to dig inside ourselves and find fresh reserves of gratitude and positivity when we feel that the world is closing in around us. When we take a moment to remember how much goodness our life holds and how very blessed we are, we find the optimism that propels us forward into change.

In my life, when I feel fear, shame, and despair, I work hard to find some small sense of gratitude. We all make a choice, every single day, about how we interpret our circumstances. Life is filled with so much goodness and wonder, and the happiest people remain grateful even in the face of setbacks. If nothing bad ever happened to us, we wouldn't be able to appreciate all the good in our life, and we certainly wouldn't have the opportunity to grow.

When you start to feel overwhelmed by your circumstances, look around and remember, you are not alone. We are all facing struggles of our own. When you look past your own troubles and reach a hand out to someone else, you'll both feel better.

In Summary—Rising to the Occasion

In the middle of my divorce, my optimism was tested. I certainly had my days of thinking that I would never marry again and never find someone who would be a good fit with me—let's face it, I am not the easiest person to live with. I tried hard not to worry about the future too much (very unlike me) and just focused on getting through each week as best I could. If I lingered too long on my thoughts about who I might be in the future, I imagined a lonely woman living alone, with an unhealthy interest in wine and a sizable jigsaw puzzle collection.

Not long after my divorce, I struck up a conversation with a man named David when he sat next to me on an airplane. After our flight we stayed in touch, exchanging emails a few times a month, and it was clear that we had a connection. After about six months, we decided to meet again and have dinner in a city where we were both headed for work. The week before our dinner, I was nervous but excited to see him again. Then, the night before our date, I had a minor panic attack. I hadn't been on a date in nearly twenty years. The idea of starting over again with someone new and different felt overwhelming.

I called my best friend, who talked me back to reality. She said, "It's a dinner, nothing more. Go and enjoy it, and don't add pressure on yourself that doesn't need to be there." I felt a thousand times better. It actually turned out to be a great date, which led to a long-term, serious, long-distance relationship. David is a successful businessman and has had a huge positive influence on my life. He has restored my optimism in relationships and marriage and my belief in the possibilities for business and success. I am so glad I remained open to the possibility of falling in love with someone new, even as uncomfortable as it was.

There is stress associated with awakening each morning to a problem that has yet to be resolved or even a goal you've set for yourself but not yet reached. You need the *motivation* to attack a problem from a new perspective and the *optimism* to believe that the steps you take on this new day will bring you closer to your objective . . . even if it's a small, incremental move in the right direction.

The path of pain and hardship is not one you'd take by choice, but when you push yourself out of your comfort and disengagement zones, you better prepare yourself to be resilient. If you're not in crisis right now but are taking proactive steps toward growing out of your comfort zone, cultivating a healthy optimism can empower you to achieve your goals. Rising to the occasion takes a conscious decision. The choice is yours to either accept the adventure or remain in the comfort of your status quo.

Keeping your own optimism appropriately high helps you see the best in your situation, allows you to maintain hope for the future, and reminds you to be grateful for the gifts and strengths you hold inside you right now. Please trust me on this: You are capable of so much more than you know.

Endnotes

1　Martin E. P. Seligman, *Learned Optimism* (New York: Knopf, 1991), 4–5.

2　Michael Chaiton et al., "Estimating the Number of Quit Attempts It Takes to Quit Smoking Successfully in a Longitudinal Cohort of Smokers," *BMJ Open* 6, 1 (2016), http://dx.doi.org/10.1136/bmjopen-2016-011045.

3　Daniel Goleman and Richard E. Boyatzis, "Social Intelligence and the Biology of Leadership," *Harvard Business Review*, September 2008, https://hbr.org/2008/09/social-intelligence-and-the-biology-of-leadership.

CHAPTER 6

Stress Tolerance: Building Your Stamina

Nobody's life is entirely free of stress, and, believe it or not, that's a good thing. Stress keeps us in motion, nudging us out of our comfort zone and helping us grow. It serves as a powerful catalyst, prodding us toward positive change. Successfully coping with stress builds our confidence, too, so we're better prepared to face the bigger challenges that may come our way.

Just as weight lifting causes your muscles to develop small tears, which your body eventually repairs into bigger, stronger muscles, stress may sometimes feel like it's tearing you down. As with your abdominals and your glutes, though, the right amount of stress—not too little, not too much—builds your confidence muscles. An ability to tolerate stress is important no matter what your life looks like right now. It's especially important when you are facing an exit out of your comfort zone, whether that exit has been imposed on you or you've chosen it.

Our ability to tolerate stress slides on a continuum. Imagine it as a ruler with a green band on one end, yellow in the middle, and red on the other end. When you're in the green band, you're calm and at ease, and you're coping effectively with whatever stressors you're facing. When you enter the yellow zone, it's a warning that you need to step back and recharge so you can cope better with stress. You'll know you're in the yellow zone if you start feeling frazzled and short tempered or especially anxious. When you edge into the red zone, you're in panic mode. You're facing more stressors than you know how to handle, and you need help.

Everyone's ruler is different. I know people who have a narrow band of stress tolerance—any change can rattle them—and others who have a wide band, which means they can handle a number of stressful events at once without losing their cool or becoming less productive. What is your endurance for stress? Are you able to take problems in stride, or does an unexpected roadblock throw you off course? Use your EQ to *recognize* where you are in terms of stress tolerance and *read* situations that provide opportunities to strengthen your ability to cope with stressors. The goal is to keep the green band on your ruler as wide as possible, so you have solid reserves in place to support you when you need them most.

We all have warning signals that tell us when we are heading into the red band. For me, the first sign is forgetfulness. I get home from a trip and unpack my suitcase, only to discover I left a pair of shoes in the hotel closet. I grab dinner during an airport layover, then get on the plane and realize my jacket is still draped over my chair at the restaurant. I have left phone and computer chargers in hotels and offices scattered across the United States. Many people leave things behind. *I only do it when my stress tolerance has hit a critical low.* It is like my own personal warning light, telling me that I need to stop and deal with my stress level before something really bad happens.

Your stress signal is probably completely different than mine. Maybe you lose your temper more easily when you're too far into your red band. Maybe you start fueling yourself with too much chocolate and caffeine, or you have trouble sleeping. When you notice that you're starting to head into your red band, don't just try to push through the stress. Listen to what your EQ is telling you, and take a step back. Give yourself some breathing space and a chance to recharge by going for a run, meeting a friend for a cup of coffee, or staying off email for the weekend. If all you can manage is a few minutes to relax, take a quick walk or do some stretching. I promise you, you'll come back to your problems stronger and more in control.

Applying the Three *R*s to Stress Tolerance

- When it comes to stress tolerance, it is important to *recognize* your own symptoms of anxiety or fatigue.

- When *reading* your environment, make a distinction between tasks that are urgent and those that are important, so you can prioritize accordingly.
- *Respond* to your rising stress levels by taking a self-imposed time-out or negotiating for extended deadlines, additional resources, or a changed workload.
- Each time you develop a new stress coping mechanism, you'll find yourself moving forward with a greater level of resilience.

The time you spend in the discomfort zone of your grid is valuable and productive. That's where the stress occurs, but it's also where the magic happens. You're taking on risks, wrestling with challenges, and giving yourself the opportunity to succeed and grow. With challenge comes stress, and to be effective outside your comfort zone, you need to be able to handle that stress. Stress tolerance is a vital emotional intelligence skill because it provides you with a tool kit for coping. It gives you perspective, so you don't overreact when things go wrong. It helps you stay healthier, because stress tolerance helps control anxiety and its physical side effects, like high blood pressure. It helps you get comfortable with adversity, and when you do, the green band on your ruler becomes wider. In turn, you increase your ability to take on risks, meet goals, and launch into the confidence zone.

Stress tolerance is also connected to increased self-control. The days you are the most stressed out are probably the days you're more touchy, agitated, and short tempered. As a result, little irritations that might not normally bother you become so annoying that you might snap back at someone. Or say something sarcastic you'll later regret. Or completely shut down. Or cry. In short, you are more likely to be triggered. When you keep your tolerance for stress high, you also keep your emotional control high, by default. That's good for you *and* the people around you.

Bulking Up Your Stress Tolerance

Building on our earlier metaphor, picture stress tolerance as a muscle. If you don't use it, it atrophies, and you lose the ability to handle even small bumps in the road calmly and with confidence. But exercise that muscle, and it grows stronger. Just like with weight lifting, when you repeatedly push your stress tolerance muscles right to their limit, that limit expands. You're able to tackle more challenges and take them in stride.

You wouldn't run a marathon without training for it, would you? So don't try to run the marathon of life without building up the strength and endurance you'll need to get through it with grace and enjoyment. The best way to bulk up your stress tolerance is to take on small challenges, a little at a time. Think of them as baby steps out of the comfort zone. Each success will push that green band on your ruler a little bit wider. Your confidence will grow, until eventually you know for certain that you're strong enough to cope with whatever life throws your way.

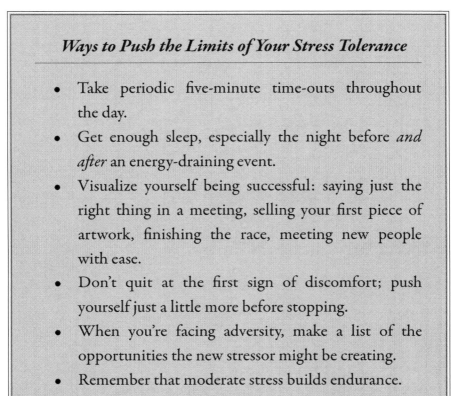

Ways to Push the Limits of Your Stress Tolerance

- Take periodic five-minute time-outs throughout the day.
- Get enough sleep, especially the night before *and after* an energy-draining event.
- Visualize yourself being successful: saying just the right thing in a meeting, selling your first piece of artwork, finishing the race, meeting new people with ease.
- Don't quit at the first sign of discomfort; push yourself just a little more before stopping.
- When you're facing adversity, make a list of the opportunities the new stressor might be creating.
- Remember that moderate stress builds endurance.

When you're training for a marathon, you have to give it everything you've got, adding more and more miles to your practice runs. But you don't train like that every day—if you did, you'd collapse before you ever made it to the race. Instead, you mix rest days into your schedule to let your muscles rebuild. (See the example below for an illustration of how these phases of training flow in the quadrant model.)

The Quadrant Model Applied to a Marathon Training Plan

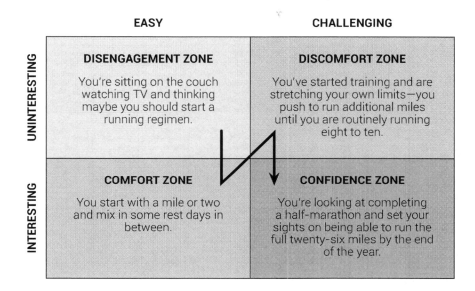

Your stress tolerance muscles are no different. It's important to push them to their limit—but then you need to give them a chance to rest and recoup. As you're working hard in your confidence and discomfort zones, your EQ can help you recognize when you're starting to move past the boundaries of your stress tolerance. This is the moment to move back into the comfort zone to recharge, before you wear yourself out and start to exhibit the stress signals we talked about earlier. Then, when you've replenished your stress tolerance, you can head back over to the other side of the model again.

Eating healthily, exercising, and making sure you get enough sleep help keep your stress tolerance high, and so does setting aside time for things you enjoy. You might recharge by knitting, reading, playing in a softball league, doing yoga, going to the movies, or getting a glass of wine or a cup of tea with a friend. The key is to make sure each day includes something that relaxes you, even for just a few minutes. When I'm under stress, I like to do jigsaw puzzles. I find them relaxing, and they serve as a small problem I can solve easily and feel good about. Time with my family and with my more optimistic friends helps, too.

If you have a job that includes vacation time, make a commitment that you will use it all, every year. Even better, on those days off, don't check your work email or your voicemail even once. (I know it's hard, but you can do it!) So many women I know say they are overworked and tired, but most of them don't stop working on the weekends or during vacations. In full disclosure, I am guilty of this myself. Because I run my own company, I feel responsible for making sure everything flows smoothly, and I don't have a big staff to take care of my business when I am out of the office.

This is one area where my boyfriend, David, has helped me grow a lot. We live three thousand miles apart, and being the chronic planner and organizer I am, I want to sync our calendars, purchase airline tickets for our visits in advance, and know where I will be way ahead of time. David is the exact opposite. He likes to wait until the last minute and figure out the details as he goes. Early in our relationship, his spontaneous, eleventh-hour decision making *really* stressed me out. I had never operated that way before, and it was very uncomfortable for me. I realized that I needed to make a choice: end the relationship on the grounds that I could not be expected to be so flexible, or decide to accept that I wouldn't have so much control over my time or travel plans and adapt accordingly. I chose to be adaptable.

Despite my initial anxiety, what I have discovered about letting go is that I enjoy myself much more than I thought I would. I am not overscheduled every day the way I used to be. During our time together, David and I have discovered things by wandering around life, both figuratively and literally. I have had adventures that I would never have found with my old ways. I have learned that I am not indispensable and that life is more negotiable than I realized. I now realize that my nervous tension in the beginning of the relationship was self-imposed, and I was wasting my energy by worrying about pretty insignificant things.

This is the opposite of what I thought would happen when I let go of some control. Surprisingly, living with more spontaneity has lowered my anxiety. I don't fret as much over things that really don't matter, and I am more relaxed and present to experience things as they happen. I know I made a good choice.

So the next time you find yourself saying you can't afford to take some unplanned or impulsive time off to decompress, ask yourself, "Can I afford not to?" When you refill your stress tolerance bank, you're making deposits that you can later use to fund your career advancement, personal growth, and family happiness.

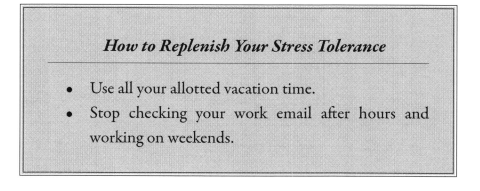

How to Replenish Your Stress Tolerance

- Use all your allotted vacation time.
- Stop checking your work email after hours and working on weekends.

- Remember you are not alone; don't be afraid to turn to others for help.
- Get outside: The fresh air will help clear your head and give you a new perspective.
- Prepare your body to handle stress by eating healthily and getting plenty of sleep.
- Make exercising a regular part of your routine, and increase the chances of sticking with it by doing something you love (be creative!).
- Cultivate a hobby that you can enjoy on weekends or a few times a month.
- Practice gratitude. Make it a habit to reflect each day on the good in your life and everything you have to be thankful for.

The Power of Perspective

As you begin to push yourself out of your comfort zone and into your confidence zone, a nifty side effect occurs: You gain perspective. After a health scare, having a mouse in the house just isn't that traumatic. I have friends who are very easily rattled by what I think are little things: a flat tire, an offensive Facebook post, a change in the school schedule, a new computer at work, a fender bender.

I once spoke with a woman who had taken an EQ assessment and scored relatively low on it, especially in stress tolerance. I asked her about the types of situations that created the most stress for her, and she said, "Well, I just haven't been the same since my near-death experience."

I was surprised and concerned for her, and I considered that her low stress tolerance score might very well be justified.

"Tell me what happened," I implored.

She told me that she had been entering the freeway, attempting to merge into traffic. Her entry lane was ending, but there was an eighteen wheeler on her left and a wall to her right. She didn't judge her speed well enough and realized she was running out of lane, so she slowed down to let the truck pass, but she could tell that the driver wouldn't be able to pull ahead fast enough to allow her passing room.

I closed my eyes, imagining what she was going to say next. I pictured her car squeezed between the truck and the freeway barrier wall, glass shattering everywhere and the car mangled around her, firemen cutting her out of the car and Life Flight racing her to the hospital in critical condition.

She said, "Well, the tail of the truck's trailer caught my rear bumper and pulled it completely off."

I asked, "Did you lose control of the car?"

She said, "No."

I asked, "Did it break any of your windows?"

She said, "No. But I had to pull over on a busy freeway and wait for a tow truck. It was terrifying."

Now, I don't mean to minimize what was obviously a scary situation for her, but a "near-death experience"? I think not.

When we don't expand ourselves and add challenge regularly,

eventually everyday life may become overwhelming. Don't let this happen to you! I would hate for you to find yourself hesitant to venture to the grocery store, scared of what lurks around every corner.

When you lose perspective and become afraid to take even the smallest risks, you miss out on so much enjoyment and satisfaction, but you may find there are other side effects, too. Your loved ones may hesitate to turn to you for support, and you might find that there's also a negative impact on your professional reputation.

My employees and I once ran a training program for the sales team of a Fortune 50 company, helping them refine their sales process. We were conducting a common exercise in sales training: videotaping each salesperson as he or she gave a quick overview of the company and the product they sold, so we could review the tapes later and provide feedback. The company had locations across the United States, so we were running the training as a series of regional meetings.

At one of these regional meetings, we arrived at the conference room and were told that one of the participants had locked herself in her hotel room and was refusing to come down to the session. She was so terrified of being videotaped that she had barricaded herself upstairs.

I had a hard time understanding the woman's resistance. She was in sales, so she gave presentations in front of customers every day. I suggested a more private option—that we videotape her in a separate room, without her boss and her coworkers watching her, to see if that lessened her anxiety. But the idea was so stressful that she wouldn't even come down and talk to us about the options—she was having a complete breakdown.

In the end, we called her husband, and he had to fly out to pick her up. She just would not leave the hotel room without him. I am guessing that she had more going on in her life than we knew, and the pressure of the video was the tipping point for her. Without a sufficiently wide band of stress tolerance, she risked her reputation and quite possibly her job.

Our own experiences aren't the only ones to give us perspective, either. When we use our EQ to look beyond our own tensions and anxiety and observe the challenges the people around us are facing, we typically see our problems in a whole new light. A healthy dose of perspective can remind us that everyone struggles with something and can fill us with gratitude for our many blessings.

After Steve and I divorced, I continued living in our family home, in a rural neighborhood in New Hampshire. It was intimidating for me to consider living on my own out in the country with limited city-provided services, but I decided that if I could tough it out even for one year, it would be easier on my kids not to have to move.

The first Thanksgiving after our divorce, it was my year to have the kids with me for the holiday, and my sister and her children were arriving from out of state to spend the long weekend with us. On the day before Thanksgiving, we got hit with a very big snowstorm. Because many of the trees were still covered in leaves and we hadn't really had a hard frost, it was disastrous. Most of the trees collapsed under the weight of the heavy snow, which caught on the branches in a tangle of leaves, and when they fell over, they knocked power lines down with them. Our water comes from a well on our property, which requires an electric pump, so when I lose power, I lose water, too.

I had lived in the house for about eight years and had lost power before. Usually, when this happened, we checked into a hotel or stayed with friends who had a generator. But because this was a holiday weekend, the few local hotels were already full, and most of my neighbors already had houseguests.

With just such a situation in mind, I had bought a small emergency generator the winter before. I figured I could use that to supply power to the essential appliances (the furnace, well pump, refrigerator, oven, and a few lights), which would be sufficient until our power was restored. With a little luck and a heavy dose of optimism, I set forth a plan to make a modest Thanksgiving dinner.

Let me describe for you what is involved in using a temporary generator. I had to drag the hundred-pound unit from my garage out to the driveway so it had good ventilation and start it up. Then I had to go down to my basement to switch the master power on my electric box to generator power and individually select the fuses to switch on without overloading the generator. At night, I had to follow the process in the complete dark, when it was ten degrees outside. The generator ran on gasoline, and the tank only held enough to run for about six hours, so each night I had to turn everything off, snuggle the family under blankets, and switch the main power back to the utility in the hope that the power company would restore our electricity overnight.

We did okay for about three days. But by the third night, after going through my whole routine, I was lying alone in my cold bed in the dark, and I just started sobbing. I felt overwhelmed and kept saying to myself, "Who do you think you are to imagine you could run this house all on your own?" Time to make some choices. I planned to call a realtor the next day. Then I started worrying about my limited housing options, because apartments in my area are hard to find, and there are virtually no rental homes. I felt pressure to stay in town so my kids wouldn't have to change schools (Steve had moved out of the district), and all of it just made me cry harder.

Then I started thinking about a friend of mine who had two young children, who were two and four years old. The month earlier, she had shared with me that her husband had been caught with child pornography at work. Naturally, it was devastating news. As a result, he was brought in for questioning by the local police department, the family computers were seized, and the children spent the next week in meetings with child psychologists to assess whether there had been any abuse. The whole situation had caught my friend completely by surprise and was quite shocking. He lost his job, and my friend, who was a stay-at-home mom, was suddenly forced to face a divorce, his possible jail time, a job search for herself, the challenge of explaining to her kids and the community what had happened, and probably a move from her home.

I started to think about what her Thanksgiving weekend had been like compared with mine, and I felt so much empathy for her. That dose of perspective was all it took to slap my self-pity in the face, and immediately my situation didn't seem quite so overwhelming. Once again, I realized that I had much to be grateful for and was reminded that I would overcome this inconvenient but very temporary period in my life by choosing to be resilient.

The Stress Management Toolbox

One of the keys to stress tolerance is to have a toolbox of coping techniques ready at all times. I have a few favorites that I rely on, and you might find them helpful, too.

Staying Organized

My first line of defense against stress is more of a preventative measure. I have found that keeping my environment reasonably orderly reduces mental clutter, eliminates the last-minute panic of not being able to find the things I need, and gives me a wider green band of stress tolerance.

With a busy professional life and two teenagers in the house, I know how tough staying organized can be, but I promise you, it's worth it. When you're not scrambling to find missing soccer schedules and permission slips and you can make dinner without having to shift piles of paperwork just to free up some counter space, you might be surprised by the clarity of mind organization brings. You're able to focus on the day ahead of you while getting ready for work, instead of digging through your closet for the black boots you *know* are in there somewhere.

Now, I work out of my home when I'm not traveling, and I will be the first to tell you that my home office is pretty disorganized—I have piles of stuff pretty much everywhere. So I don't mean to say you need a Martha Stewart–worthy home, but having to look for things at the last minute can waste a ton of time and add unnecessary stress when you are trying to get out the door. Seeing a clean room, an orderly closet, or an uncluttered kitchen just *feels good.* Like the feeling of clean sheets.

You can hire someone to help you get things under control, or you can enjoy the sense of accomplishment and pride you get when you look at the garage, knowing you were the one to face the spiders and old bikes and create order from mayhem. And when you're done, you might even be able to park your car in the garage! That will save time (and stress) in the mornings, because you won't have to warm up the car and clear it of ice or snow, and you'll save time at the car wash because it will stay cleaner longer.

I can appreciate the fact that getting and staying organized can be challenging. Some of us have the best intentions and never get to it, while the rest of us do get organized, only to find that the entropy of life quickly washes it all away. Again, perfection is not the goal as much as progress. Set an intention to stay organized, and then do your best to make it happen by creating a structure and a schedule for success. Mark organization time on your calendar, and keep the appointment with yourself (or be sure to reschedule right away), or hire someone to come regularly to make sure it happens. Instead of saying that you don't have the time or the money (keep reading for more on finances), remind yourself that you are making deposits into your stress tolerance bank.

Compartmentalization

People usually think of compartmentalization as unhealthy. We tend to see it as a robotic approach to life, and we think of people as emotionally disconnected and lacking integration skills when they compartmentalize. If your husband had to lay off a handful of employees, then came home from work, changed out of his suit, and started cheerfully goofing around with your kids, you might think he felt no guilt or pain about putting people out of work.

Over the years, though, I've found that compartmentalization can actually be a highly effective coping strategy. It's probable that your husband is very upset by the layoff—you know he's a good person. But when he came home, he set aside his "boss" identity, just like he set aside his work clothes. By shutting the door on that part of his life, just for a little while, he's allowing himself to be fully present at home, in roles that make him happy. This helps him regroup and recharge so he can face the next workday with renewed strength. It's unhealthy to overcompartmentalize—that is, detach too completely—but, used properly, compartmentalization can be an excellent coping tool.

As you've learned, my life is very full, and I have a number of roles. I am a mother to two girls who are now teenagers, I am a road warrior, I am a daughter of two parents and two stepparents. I am a sister and a stepsister, a granddaughter, an ex-wife, a business owner, a fiancée, and an author. You probably have at least as many roles in your own life, including some other very important ones, like caregiver to an aging parent, volunteer, or church member. Earlier in my life, I didn't put much thought into the diversity of my roles; they blended together, and I just thought of them as my life. But during my most difficult days, I remember just how helpful compartmentalization can be.

During various periods in my life I have been consumed by financial worries, marital woes, business challenges, and family conflict. But when I sit down in an executive coaching session with a client, I can narrow my focus down to just that person. Everything else falls away, and for an hour or two I am in my confidence zone, working hard and getting an energy boost from accomplishing something challenging. Then, when I go back to my family, I can take that energy with me and be better equipped to handle whatever the day holds. By approaching each situation mindfully and being fully present, I am able to ban the nagging script that is running in the background of my mind. I'm sure you have your own loop of worry that seems to be on constant repeat.

When I try to shut out all that noise and put my energy on the task at hand, I am better. I write higher-quality proposals, I am a better trainer because I can be present enough with my audience to adapt spontaneously to their nuanced needs, and when I am done with my work, I leave with renewed energy. Instead of feeling drained or overwhelmed, I feel strong. Fueled by the feeling of accomplishment, I am able to switch gears and approach the next task on my to-do list with singular focus. I can enjoy trips with my daughters and time with David when I leave the mobile phone at home, along with the list of work tasks that need to be accomplished, and I bask in my undivided time with them. And they appreciate that I give them my full attention.

The Worst-Case/Best-Case Scenario

If the other strategies fail and I'm fighting against some serious stress, I often turn to the third tool in my stress tolerance toolbox, the "worst-case/best-case scenario" game. When I start falling into a spiral of worry and anxiety, I pause that negative cycle by asking myself, "What's the very worst that could happen? And if that does happen, what would I do about it?" This trick is a great way to take a step back and calm yourself down. Once you play the scenario out, you'll usually find that even the worst outcome has a plausible response that you're equipped to handle. What happens may not be ideal, but few things are truly life or death.

If the woman at my sales training had been able to calm down enough to think about the worst-case scenario, she might have been able to choose her response very differently. She would have realized that the very worst thing that could happen was that she might embarrass herself (which she did anyway, by barricading herself in her room!). Even if she watched the video and thought she was terrible, it wouldn't have hurt her professionally, since there were no customers in the room. It wouldn't have cost her any sales (it might even have gained her some). But I didn't have a chance to work through this thought process with her, because she wouldn't leave her room—or her comfort zone.

Like most of you probably do, I start with the worst-case side because fear pushes me to assume a terrible outcome. We buy insurance because we want to be covered in case of a disaster. We sign contracts and guarantees in case something goes wrong. David has taught me a very important corollary: the best-case scenario game. He has helped me realize that so often, we don't plan for success nearly as well as we prepare for failure.

If that same saleswoman had turned her focus on the best-case scenario, she would have realized that the information she could learn about herself through the sales training would only have helped her improve her sales effectiveness. In turn, this could have resulted in more sales, which would have led to higher commissions and more positive recognition for her at the company. There are two potential outcomes to every choice we make, and we can base our choice on fear or on potential.

The next time you find yourself worrying about the future, try playing the worst-case/best-case scenario game. Maybe you're due for a mammogram and you're so nervous about going that you keep putting off making the appointment. Take a step back and ask yourself, "If I have the test, what's the very worst that could happen?" Yes, the doctor might find a lump—but then you could start treatment right away instead of letting it grow. And what's the likelihood that will happen? On the best-case side, it's much more probable that you'll leave the appointment with a clean bill of health, especially if you have no family history of cancer, and you'll have a lot less to worry about. No matter what the outcome is, though, you're choosing to face any discomfort with strength instead of fear.

Stop Blocking Your Own Exit

When pushing yourself into moderate challenge, save your stress reserves for learning new things, solving new problems, coping with the anxiety that comes with change, stretching yourself to adapt to a new schedule or routine, and deepening your relationships with others. Removing ongoing stressors makes sense because it gives you a wider band of tolerance. But if you're like most people, myself included, there's probably an area of your life where you're creating unnecessary stress for yourself.

Maybe you have a habit of overscheduling yourself and ending up double booked. Maybe you put off dealing with minor problems until they reach crisis level. Maybe you growl at your colleagues or loved ones when you are stressed. It's only human to react like this sometimes, but it does add bumps on the road out of your comfort zone. Take a minute to think about what your own personal pitfall might be, and how you can set a new habit. When we create additional stress for ourselves, we're throwing up roadblocks in front of our on-ramp to the confidence zone, without even realizing it.

We all have our own unique roadblocks, but over time I've come to see some common threads. As women, we sometimes feel we need to be able to "do it all," and we create stress for ourselves by not relying on help when we need it. I have a friend who hires a housekeeper to clean her house twice a month. I invited her to have coffee with me one morning, and she said, "I can't. My housekeeper is coming today, and I need to clean the house for her."

I have another friend who desperately needs a housekeeper (we are talking borderline hoarder), and she won't hire one because she says her house is too dirty. I am pretty sure the point of having a housekeeper is for that person to come to a dirty house, so what gives? So often, we make an effort to accept help when we need it, but we fall short of the finish line by not being able to let go completely. We've got to let go of perfection in order to proceed. Otherwise, we'll spend a lifetime stuck in the comfort zone, feeling dissatisfied or even miserable.

Another huge source of stress for so many people I know is money. Keeping your finances organized is critical, including not procrastinating on balancing the checkbook. Now, I have certainly had my own hardships when it comes to money. In 2009, Steve and I had over $150,000 in tax, consumer, and business debt, and we were late on our mortgage, with no equity and not a dollar in savings, including for retirement. The burden of that pressure and fear was tremendous. Our problems were the result of a bad economy but, even more than that, bad financial habits. We considered filing for bankruptcy, but chose instead to face our problem head on and work our way out of debt through new discipline and a lot of hard work. This choice was not easy to make, and Steve and I had different opinions on how to proceed, which put more strain on our marriage.

For me, staying in the comfort zone could have meant just making the monthly minimum payments on the credit cards and never managing to get out of debt. It could have meant walking away from the house and letting the bill collectors try to find us. It could have meant avoiding the IRS and delaying facing the consequences for as long as possible. Any of those responses might have been more comfortable in the short term, but I knew they would be more painful in the long run. So, we called the IRS and worked out a payment plan, and we agreed not to get into any more tax debt. We enrolled in a debt management program for the consumer debt. We worked out a monthly payment plan for the business debt. And, eventually, we got ourselves free.

How did we do it? We ate at home every night, ended our daily fancy coffee run, and drove our cars until they had over 100,000 miles each. We cut back on cable, changed phone companies, and reduced our household and business expenses to the bare minimum. We didn't take any vacations, and I didn't buy new clothes (honestly, that was the hardest!). I had a goal in mind and was motivated to achieve it.

In the end, that discipline paid off: By 2012, we had reduced our total debt to $24,000. By 2014, it was completely paid off. And while I was fighting to get out from under all that debt, another interesting thing happened . . . I got a taste of resilience in the confidence zone. Because of the desperation of my situation, I took more risks. I raised my rates for client work, instead of trying to entice clients with discounts. I negotiated for travel expense reimbursement and fees for things I normally did pro bono. And every time I got what I asked for, it empowered me to try again. The success validated my worth, and every dollar I earned was buying my freedom.

I have since survived a 30 percent pay cut, a divorce, and an expensive out-of-state relationship with David without incurring more debt. I didn't manage this through some financial windfall like a lottery win or an inheritance; I have just been disciplined and consistent. I am not sharing this very embarrassing part of my story to tell you that I am anything special. If I can do it, you can too. If you are willing to get out of your comfort zone and work through the discomfort zone, you will make it to the amazing confidence zone with the power of resilience in action.

For you, that may mean getting a different job, taking on a second job, or going back to work if you aren't working now. It may mean using more EQ, particularly self-control, to keep your spending in check. If you need to upgrade your job skills to make more money, you'll find an ample supply of free courses online. The only thing holding you back is the fear of leaving what is familiar. Trust me, not having financial stress will change your life and build your stress tolerance, so you can spend more time in the confidence zone, living life the way you desire it to be.

In Summary—Moderate Stress Builds Tolerance

No one's life is free of stress. Maybe you have been caught off guard by a surprise crisis, like I was. Or maybe you're in a time of self-directed growth right now. Even if you've been fortunate enough to have never had your world rocked by true crisis, it is better to build more tolerance now, so you're prepared when the unexpected happens. Stress tolerance also helps you navigate your days with more poise and joy. By building your reserves of stamina, you empower yourself to get through life's challenges more resiliently.

Not all stress is the same. Avoiding it can hurt you just as much as an extended stay in the red zone. To become more tolerant, use your EQ to monitor your own stress levels. It will help gauge when you need to tap into your motivation and optimism to tolerate more and when you need to step off the gas and coast for a while. We can all endure much more than we realize, and our behavioral responses are completely in our control. In fact, with so much in our life out of our control, doesn't it make sense to own the only thing we can . . . our choices?

CHAPTER 7

Super Survivors

One of the goals of this book is to help you learn to empower yourself in your life, across any and every circumstance—when you are stuck in a comfort zone rut, afraid to make a change, or when you are faced with challenges that have launched you from safety. I hope this book will help you build the skills you need to take an emotionally intelligent path instead of letting the things that happen to you derail or destroy you. My aim is to help you take risks and build your confidence, so you can create the life you desire.

No one's life goes exactly as planned: There are bumps in every road, and, at some point, everyone faces problems. For most of this book, our focus has been on preparing for and coping with the typical struggles we all face at home or at work—job loss, illness, divorce, the upheaval of a move or a new baby. Humans are strong and adaptable, and we have the ability to handle these challenges. But within this capable general population is an even more impressive group of people, often referred to as "Super Survivors."

Super Survivors haven't just coped with tragedy but have actually used it to become stronger. They discovered an incredible inner strength as a result of being pushed to their limits, and they used that strength to build a rich and meaningful life out of the ashes of tragedy. These Super Survivors all share a set of traits that made them more resilient in the face of disaster. As I reflect on their ongoing drive to overcome physical and psychological traumas, my humble struggles seem minor in comparison to their stories of hardship.

Super Survivors have high optimism about their own ability to rebound from tragedy, but they have no delusions about the world or what happened to them.[1] They are realistic about the problems they face, but rather than wallowing in self-pity, they get to work on the process of healing. Many Super Survivors devote themselves to hard work as a way to channel the negative things that happened to them into something more positive. They often dedicate their life to helping people in similar circumstances. This gives them a sense of control, allowing them to write the next chapters of their story for themselves.

Pessimists allow a tragic event to define their future. Optimists see the tragic event as a point in time; although they cherish the life they lived before, they are able to accept their present condition. Acceptance is the choice they make that creates the opportunity to redefine themselves. Resilience is the outcome.

Instead of dwelling on the tragic event, optimists focus on the possibility for future happiness. Their real growth comes from the adversity they face in their recovery. Think about our own collective experience as a country after the events of September 11, 2001. We were shocked and scared, but the optimists among us channeled that fear into a sense of gratitude for everything America stands for: democracy, liberty, courage, and resilience. We used that horrific experience to immediately become better citizens and community members, reaching out to our neighbors for comfort, donating money to aid the rescue operations, and doing whatever we could to help those affected by the tragedy.

When I'm facing adversity, I draw strength and encouragement from the stories of these Super Survivors. Knowing that they are able to *survive* their awful circumstances and also continue to *thrive* reminds me that I can too. I'd like to share with you a few of the stories that have inspired me the most. They help me remember the gift of gratitude—and how the simple act of appreciating what we have now will provide us with a sense of abundance and security. When you understand how wealthy you really are—in friends, in health, in family, in surroundings, and in other resources—you start to realize that you are taken care of today and that you will be tomorrow, as well.

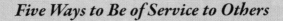

Five Ways to Be of Service to Others

1. Find online discussion boards or Facebook groups that deal with the same issues you have faced and contribute to them (you can do this anonymously).
2. Attend support group meetings and offer help.
3. Start a blog to share your stories of both struggle and solutions that worked for you.
4. Volunteer your time to work with others in need.
5. Tell your story; until you do, you deny others the chance to identify and learn from you. It also helps them to know they aren't the only ones who have struggled with similar issues.

Michael J. Fox

Michael J. Fox was already a well-known actor with the promise of a long, successful career ahead of him when he was diagnosed with Parkinson's disease at just twenty-nine years old. He refused to let his disease slow him down, though: He continued to work, starring in a TV show and then, when his disease progressed, doing voice-over work. He established the Michael J. Fox Foundation for Parkinson's Research and has been a tireless advocate for efforts to cure the disease.

Despite all the challenges he has faced, Mr. Fox titled his memoir *Lucky Man*, because that's how he sees himself: blessed with a loving family, meaningful work, and a cause to fight for.[2] He "has spoken and written extensively about his predisposition to look at challenges, including his Parkinson's disease, through a lens of optimism and humor. His message has always been one of gratitude for the support he has received from his fellow Parkinson's patients, and hope and encouragement for every decision to take action—no matter how big or small—to help advance the pursuit of a cure."[3]

My grandfather died of Parkinson's disease, so I have witnessed firsthand the struggles of those who live with it. I imagine having to cope with the disease while remaining in the public eye must be even more challenging, yet Michael J. Fox has embraced his condition and stayed visible and active when it might have been easier to leave his acting career behind and live more privately.

We can only guess at what has driven him to continue his acting career and become a leader in Parkinson's advocacy, but his dedication to his family and to the needs of other people with Parkinson's disease seem to be powerful motivators. Rather than using his diagnosis as an excuse to give up and retire to his armchair, he has found new sources of motivation to keep him engaged in meaningful work. We can all learn from his powerful example.

Elizabeth Smart

Elizabeth Smart was just fourteen years old when she was kidnapped from her Salt Lake City home, abducted in the middle of the night while her family slept. Her kidnappers held her hostage for nine months, forcing her to endure torture, rape, and starvation. But in the years since her rescue, she has not just healed but used her newfound strength to help others. She created the Elizabeth Smart Foundation to prevent crimes against children and help survivors of sexual abuse. She fell in love and got married. She even published a memoir, to share with others the lessons she has learned in her healing process.

In her memoir, Ms. Smart wrote, "As of this writing, I am twenty-five years old. I have been alive for 307 months. Nine of those months were pretty terrible. But 298 of those months have been very good. I have been happy. I have been very blessed. Who knows how many more months I have to live? But even if I died tomorrow, nine out of 307 seems like pretty good odds."[4]

The experience she had is almost unfathomable to me, especially given that my daughters are about the age she was when she was abducted. But rather than letting it destroy her, Elizabeth Smart has managed to view the ordeal with remarkable optimism. She keeps it in perspective instead of allowing it to define her, and she remains grateful for all the blessings in her life. I am so impressed with her continued willingness to share her story, in the hope that it might help other people in their own struggles. She is a living example of optimism in action, consciously choosing resiliency and a positive outlook instead of anger and despair.

Mary Johnson

I draw a great deal of inspiration from the story of Mary Johnson, a Minneapolis woman whose only son was shot and killed in a fight that occurred at a party. The shooter, Oshea Israel, was just sixteen years old, but he was sentenced to prison for the murder.

For years, Ms. Johnson hated her son's murderer. "The root of bitterness ran deep," she said in an interview with the Forgiveness Project. "Anger had set in and I hated everyone."[5] She was a devout Christian, and it troubled her that the hatred that filled her was in conflict with her religious beliefs. Eventually, she felt ready to let go and try to forgive Mr. Israel.

Although she was afraid, she visited him in prison to tell him about her son. After talking with Mr. Israel for two hours, she hugged him and told him she forgave him. "Then, as I got up," she said, "I felt something rising from the soles of my feet and leaving me. From that day on I haven't felt any hatred, animosity, or anger. It was over."

That visit created a bond between the two that is still in place today. After serving sixteen years in prison, Oshea Israel was released when he was thirty-two years old. Mary Johnson threw him a welcome home party; now they live as neighbors, and she sees him every few days. She cares for him as a surrogate mom, and he looks out for her, too.

In an interview the two gave together, Ms. Johnson said to Mr. Oshea, "Well, my natural son is no longer here. I didn't see him graduate. Now you're going to college. I'll have the opportunity to see you graduate. . . . I didn't see him getting married. Hopefully one day, I will be able to experience that with you."[6] Ms. Johnson also cofounded an online support group with Mr. Israel's mother called From Death to Life: Two Mothers Coming Together for Healing (www.fromdeathtolife.us), dedicated to ending violence through healing and reconciliation.

What I find so impressive about Mary Johnson is her ability to accept the reality of her situation and her devastating loss, but still find good in herself and others. It must have taken a remarkable degree of stress tolerance for her to overcome the bitterness and anger of being a victim and instead use that energy to help others, even those we might think of as most undeserving of her love. This is a lady we can all learn from.

All three of these people had a choice to make: allow the tragedy to derail and destroy them, or summon their inner strength to stay motivated and optimistic.

Sam Matagi's Journey

Recently, I was fortunate enough to meet a Super Survivor named Sam Matagi. He has experienced a level of personal hardship well beyond anything I've endured in my lifetime. I interviewed him to better understand his journey as a Super Survivor.

We've talked in earlier chapters about the importance of taking small steps toward our confidence zone to prepare for the challenges we'll inevitably face, but nothing could have prepared Sam for the life-or-death circumstances that obliterated his comfort zone. On December 13, 2010, Sam's perspective on life was permanently changed.

Catapulted Into Change

On that fateful Monday morning in Kremmling, Colorado, Sam was working as a power lineman when a routine job suddenly went terribly wrong. A scrap of cut wire hit a live wire, and nearly

15,000 volts of electricity surged through his body. His hands were basically mummified.

The next thing Sam remembers is waking up on a stretcher, with the strange and surreal awareness that he was on a helicopter. The pain in his hands was excruciating, unlike anything in his memory. He was flown to the University of Colorado's burn center, and by Friday of that same week, both of his hands had been amputated to prevent the spread of infection throughout the rest of his body.

About three weeks later, when it was deemed safe for him to travel, Sam was flown to Salt Lake City to be closer to his family. He spent two days in the burn unit at the University of Utah Hospital and was then transferred to the hospital's rehabilitation center. He would need to stay there until he was able to function well on his own.

As difficult as it was to accept the permanent physical changes, Sam found that the unknown barriers and burdens he would have to overcome in the future proved to be his greatest source of fear and anxiety. The uncertainty overwhelmed him and left him with a strong sense of foreboding. For Sam, there was no path of least resistance. The road to recovery was a daily trek into uncharted territory, as he learned to accept the unthinkable: that he would never return to the comforts of life that others take for granted.

Struggling to Accept His New Reality

Sam distinctly remembers the first time he was fitted for the apparatus that was designed to replace his hands. Relating the story to me, he recalled, "I had a lot of different feelings. At first I questioned: These are supposed to replace my hands? I was bitter, then confused, and then thankful. I felt alone, like I was the only person in the world facing this problem."

Despite his own struggles, Sam was conscious of what the people around him were going through. "There were people in the room with me," he told me. "I was interested in the way they were feeling—I tried to show them things were okay. I grabbed a fork and put food in my mouth for the first time. I always worry about what other people are feeling."

Even with the prostheses, basic functions like brushing his teeth, shaving, showering, and dressing on his own had become monumental tasks. Throughout his recovery period, though, Sam was driven by the hope of returning home, to be with his family and friends. That desire motivated him to throw all his energy into rehabilitation.

On January 28, 2011, nearly two months after his accident, Sam was released from the rehabilitation center. But his excitement at returning home was tempered by a whole new set of challenges he hadn't anticipated. The staff at the center had worked hard to help Sam learn to manage life with his prosthetic hands, but he lived alone, and suddenly even the simplest tasks, like making his bed, opening doors, and cooking for himself, felt almost impossible.

The psychological and emotional impact of his injuries began to hit Sam hard at this point. Fear and self-doubt became a source of ongoing anxiety. He was overwhelmed by his inability to perform basic functions in the privacy of his own home, and the thought of venturing into the larger world was nearly incomprehensible.

Initially, Sam was unable to keep his commitment to attend continuing therapy sessions. He described feeling claustrophobic, like the rest of the world was closing in on him. He felt an overwhelming need to remain isolated. As a result, Sam began to use sleep as a means of avoiding his new reality. The therapy sessions he did manage to attend provided some level of support; however, none of the other people in his group had lost both of their hands. The uniqueness of his loss made it even harder to overcome, because he felt so alone.

At about this time, a friend invited Sam to attend a Utah Jazz basketball game. To Sam, the idea seemed completely impossible. He told his friend, "I really appreciate the invite, but I'm going to have to think about it."

Shortly after receiving the invitation, Sam attended a one-on-one session with his psychologist. During the session, the psychologist asked, "How have things been going since you've been home? Have you been able to be out and about?" Sam told him that he'd been invited to a Jazz game but that he had decided not to go.

The therapist asked, "Why don't you want to go?"

Sam said, "It's winter, and it's cold outside. I've been in the hospital for more than a month, and it was always seventy-five degrees there."

The therapist said, "How long would you have to be out in the cold?"

Sam said, "Probably twenty minutes to get there and twenty minutes to get home."

The therapist said, "Would you enjoy the game if you went?"

Sam said, "Yes."

The therapist questioned, "And how long would the game last?"

Sam said, "Probably about three hours."

The therapist replied, "Do you think you might be willing to suffer through forty minutes of cold to gain three hours of enjoyment?"

At that point, Sam realized that a small risk could bring about a considerable gain. It made sense to him. He called his friend back and accepted the invitation. At halftime, Sam went out on his own to get a burger, fries, and a drink. It was a struggle, but he overcame the fear of being watched and the possibility of dropping his food or beverage in public.

Attending the Jazz game was a major turning point in Sam's recovery. With this bold step, Sam was finally able to accept his new reality and go out in public even though he no longer had hands. This huge step outside his comfort zone required the invitation, support, and encouragement of both a concerned friend and a supportive coach. From there, Sam's motivation to enjoy himself at the game and his eventual optimism that he could handle the painful cold and the discomfort of being seen in public also helped him move toward his confidence zone. Sam was able to make it to and from the game, as well as juggle his food at halftime, in large part because of his renewed ability to tolerate stress. This was also Sam's first step toward realizing that perhaps there was a greater purpose in his misfortune.

Physical challenges continued to slow Sam's psychological recovery. One of the major obstacles people face after the loss of a limb is the ongoing condition of "phantom pain." When an injury occurs, the brain gets a pain signal from the source of the injury. In response, the brain transmits the need for nutrients and blood to that part of the body. Unfortunately, when a body part is amputated, the pain experienced before the amputation doesn't get "turned off" by the brain. In an effort to direct the healing process, the brain continues to submit signals to the missing part as though it remained connected to the body.

About 80 percent of amputees experience phantom pain, usually soon after surgery. According to the Amputee Coalition, "the length of time this pain lasts differs from person to person. It can last from seconds to minutes, to hours, to days. For most people, [it] diminishes in both frequency and duration during the first six months, but many continue to experience some level of these sensations for years."[7]

During his battle with phantom limb pain, Sam has come to believe strongly that his optimism has a direct impact on the level of pain he experiences. Over time, he has discovered a strong correlation between positive thoughts and a reduction in the intensity of his pain. During these episodes, he controls his thoughts by reflecting on the pleasant aspects of his life and his recovery. He'll think, "I have learned to drive my car again, I have an air conditioner, I have a dishwasher. I empathize with all the people in the world who don't have these same luxuries." Sam told me, "These kinds of thoughts are absolutely connected to my ability to reduce the impact and overcome the intensity of a phantom pain episode."

As you can imagine, the permanent nature of Sam's injuries has also complicated his recovery. He's unable to turn back time to the luxuries of daily living afforded to those who have the benefit of functioning limbs, and his condition places a great deal of strain on him. Over time, he has built up the stress tolerance to cope with his situation by accepting his condition and staying motivated to seek new outlets for his abilities.

Ultimately, a key breakthrough in Sam's recovery came when he started to realize that he wasn't alone in his hardship after all. As he became more adept at managing basic and complex functions with the apparatuses that have become his hands, he began to realize the extent to which he could support others who have lost one or both of their hands. Sam has become a beacon of light to those who look to him as a survivor. He now volunteers in the same recovery unit at the hospital where he was a patient during the most devastating time of his life. He listens and offers hope, sharing the light he's found on the other side of the darkness that others are currently facing.

In 2013, the Utah Red Cross honored Sam Matagi as one of their Community Heroes for his acts of exceptional courage. He was given the Good Samaritan Award for the instructional videos he has created on his vlog "The No-Handed Bandit" to help other amputees learn to use prosthetic devices. Sam continues to volunteer at the University of Utah Burn Center, counseling those who are beginning the unique journey of acceptance and recovery that has become a continuing challenge in his life.

I asked Sam what he has accomplished that he wouldn't have experienced without his injury. His response was enlightening: "There's so much, I don't even know where to begin. There are so many people I wouldn't have met . . . people I've been able to help, and people who've touched me. As much as I've helped others, they are helping me. I've gotten so many letters from students after presenting my story at their high schools. I have a huge bag full of thank you letters. One letter states, 'I was thinking of ending my life, but because of you and your story, I'm willing to fight on.'" Sam concluded, "If my life ended today, I've fulfilled my purpose."

What makes Sam's story so compelling to me? It's his continuing *motivation* to seek ways to overcome challenges. He employs a sense of *optimism* to cope with each new physical or psychological barrier that he encounters. He seeks patience and new ways to develop *stress tolerance* in order to endure the unexpected obstacles he faces each day of his life. Even with such a severe and permanent injury, Sam has found ways to be only temporarily disabled as he faces each new encounter.

In Summary—Be a Life Boat

These Super Survivors all have a strong sense of purpose and service to others. Even in the depths of despair, they remained motivated to use their experiences to help other people. They relied on their optimism to help them remember that each day would slowly get better and that they would find their way beyond struggle. They maintained a healthy stress tolerance to help them endure their pain and heal.

Perhaps the greatest takeaway from the stories of these remarkable Super Survivors is the fact that their recovery reached a significant turning point when they began focusing on the needs of others. This striking altruism is a common thread among Super Survivors. Instead of turning inward and giving in to self-pity, they direct their attention outward, concentrating on how they can help other people in similar situations. They join advocacy groups, spearhead fundraising and research efforts, speak publicly about their ordeal, and work to mentor and inspire others. Their empathy for others and their drive to be of service fuel their motivation to rise above what they've endured and promote their continued growth. They all chose resilience.

Throughout this book, we've talked about the many ways that reaching into your confidence zone can fill your life with joy and richness and help you become the best version of yourself. But the magic doesn't end there. Your newfound courage and power can be a gift to your community, as you find ways to share your talents and be of service to those around you.

Endnotes

1 David Brooks, "Tales of the Super Survivors," *New York Times,* November 24, 2015, http://www.nytimes.com/2015/11/24/opinion/tales-of-the-super-survivors.html.

2 Michael J. Fox, *Lucky Man* (New York: Bantam, 2002).

3 "Michael's Story," Michael J. Fox Foundation for Parkinson's Research, https://www.michaeljfox.org/foundation/michael-story.html.

4 Elizabeth Smart with Chris Stewart, *My Story* (New York: St. Martin's Press, 2014).

5 "Mary Johnson and Oshea Israel (USA)," Forgiveness Project, http://theforgivenessproject.com/stories/mary-johnson-oshea-israel-usa/.

6 "Forgiving Her Son's Killer: 'Not an Easy Thing,'" StoryCorps, May 20, 2011, http://www.npr.org/2011/05/20/136463363/forgiving-her-sons-killer-not-an-easy-thing.

7 "Managing Phantom Pain," Amputee Coalition, http://www.amputee-coalition.org/limb-loss-resource-center/resources-for-pain-management/managing-phantom-pain/.

CHAPTER 8

Conclusion: The Life That's Waiting for You Beyond Your Comfort Zone

We know that people with higher EQ report being happier, so if you do nothing else but focus on your EQ after reading this book, I know you will experience positive changes in your life. If you can learn to read yourself and the people around you, recognize what's needed, and respond accordingly, I'm willing to bet you'll see improvement in every aspect of your world. Your relationships are likely to get better, because you'll be interacting with people more mindfully and reflecting back what they need. Your professional life is likely to improve, because you'll be reading for opportunities to collaborate and responding to them more successfully. And you'll probably take better care of yourself, because you'll be more self-aware and in tune with your needs and emotions. All of that would be a huge accomplishment. But I'd challenge you to take it one step further.

Now that you know the importance of EQ, you can begin using it to help identify situations when a behavioral pattern starts becoming a liability—a comfort zone sticking point. It's human nature to gravitate to what's comfortable. That's why we may naturally pursue and stay with jobs and tasks that we can do easily or that we feel confident about. It is why many of us avoid conflict and resist change. But, as I've stated throughout this book, there's often a dissatisfaction that lies below the surface of our comfortable routines. We may be bothered by the knowledge that we're not reaching our full capacity to excel or anxious about our lack of personal development in a changing world. We should never let our fear of the unknown have more power than our will to choose resilience.

We all have things that we are avoiding, things that seem difficult, unappealing, or insurmountable, and yet we are unhappy because we are not addressing them. So why do we continue to dwell in that seemingly safe zone, without regard for the consequences of maintaining the status quo? Because it (sometimes) feels good, and it seems safe. And, honestly, there's nothing wrong with comfort when it isn't an inhibitor of progress. But think about it. If you want to achieve something you have never achieved before, you must *do* something you have never done before—and that's likely to feel uncomfortable.

Maybe you see yourself as someone who can be the driver of the next great initiative at your company. Are you sitting on an idea for a new and improved process or a new business venture that's been formulating in your mind? Or maybe you're thinking about taking up a new creative endeavor, like photography. Maybe you've bought the fancy, expensive camera and you spend your free time reading instructional books and scrolling through the websites of professional photographers—but that camera's still gathering dust on your desk, waiting until you feel confident enough to use it. Take a minute to ask yourself why you haven't turned your ideas and your interests into action. Are your business partners or your loved ones holding you back? How about financial limitations? Or is the real barrier your inability to take the steps that will propel you past your self-imposed limits and into the unknown?

As a Type A person, it's in my nature to want an organized, successful, and well-planned life, so I understand the desire to wait until you're fully prepared and the time is right before taking action. But if we wait until the circumstances are perfect, we'll never start. Try taking the first few baby steps toward your goal, and see what happens. Write up a business plan, and run it by a few trusted contacts. Sign up for a photography class. The momentum you'll build might be enough to keep you moving straight through the discomfort zone and into the confidence zone—that place where goals are achieved and dreams fulfilled.

Use the MOST Model to Make Positive Changes

Using your EQ to exit your comfort zone doesn't have to mean making a grand-scale, life-changing dive into dangerous, uncharted waters. Start paying attention to how you divide your time among the four quadrants (disengagement zone, comfort zone, discomfort zone, and confidence zone). When you notice that you are spending too much time on things that are easy, unproductive, or so habitual that you don't think about them anymore, you'll find yourself getting bored while you're doing them (comfort zone alert!). Consider what you have been procrastinating about, and start small (step into the discomfort zone). Pick one task or activity you've been putting off, and stay with it until it's complete (hello, confidence zone). Don't quit when it gets hard; instead, use your EQ to assess the effectiveness of your current behaviors. Determine the best steps you can take to advance your abilities and overcome the habits that are holding you back.

Maintaining a certain amount of consistency and reliability in life can support our capacity for exploring new and innovative horizons. It's okay if you need to return to the comfort zone to recharge—just don't linger there. When your energy has been restored, push back over to the challenging side. Tough it out in the discomfort zone until you reach the confidence zone again. Each time you do that, you build a wider comfort zone for yourself, giving yourself more safe space to retreat to while rebuilding your resilience.

As you continue to expand your influence, your confidence, and your sense of fulfillment, keep pursuing challenge. Push yourself a little bit each day to try something new and stretch your current skill set. You can draw on the tools in the MOST model to help you

- tap into your *motivation* and discover the reasons that make it worthwhile to get uncomfortable
- rely on your *optimism* to help you remember that good things do happen and positive change is possible
- boost your ability to withstand hardship or difficulty in a healthier way by increasing your *stress tolerance.*

When you keep nudging yourself toward things that are exciting and unfamiliar, you'll grow just a little more each day. You'll soon find that your skills and abilities are much broader than they used to be. You'll likely feel more confident and be more fulfilled—and you'll be better equipped to handle unexpected challenges that come your way.

Keep Spiraling Upward

The MOST model is a powerful tool for achieving the goals you might have laid out for yourself at the beginning of the book. We are always cycling through our four quadrants—but each time we make it into the confidence zone, we become even stronger. Our accomplishments in that zone energize us and build our motivation, increase our optimism, and bulk up our stress tolerance, so that we are even more prepared for the next cycle. Our movement through the quadrants is really a spiral, not a circle, because we are lifting ourselves up and becoming better with every loop.

I hope that you'll bravely step out of your comfort zone into your discomfort zone to do the things that scare you, the things you know you need to do if you want to grow but have been putting off. Gradually, as you build your skills and start to see success, you'll move into the confidence zone. The work is still hard, and you're still giving it everything you have, but it's rewarding and energizing.

Once you've reached your goal, you can step into the disengagement zone to catch up on all the little things that fell by the wayside while you were funneling all your time and energy into the confidence zone. When that's complete, you can head into the comfort zone for some well-deserved rest, until you're recharged and ready to start the cycle all over again. If you learn to let your EQ guide you, it can tell you when you're feeling fulfilled and when you're starting to linger too long in a particular quadrant.

Take the Leap Before You're Pushed

I'm sure you have seen the negative effects when change is *imposed* on someone. People who wait for change to be thrust upon them invariably struggle more than those who routinely invite small but notable changes into their own routines. Using your emotional intelligence will help you prepare for whatever life throws your way, and see you through it more quickly and successfully. It will also help you recognize opportunities to make progress toward goals that motivate you and keep you more fully engaged in your life.

There have been times in my life when I have stopped and said, "Wait, this is *not* the plan!" Times when my comfort zone not only kicked me out, it locked the door behind me. I didn't want to change and challenge myself, mostly because I didn't think I could. But after all these years, I have learned that struggle is good. The harder things are, the sweeter the sense of accomplishment is on the other side. I am now preparing to send one daughter off to college and make another cross-country move. As stressful as those things are, I am ready to face them with inner strength. When you begin your own journey of seeking challenge and reaching your goals, you will find that, just like me, you are much stronger than you ever realized.

A Handy Review: The Three Key Elements of EQ

1. **Recognizing yourself:** EQ involves high self-awareness about your strengths and weaknesses. It means that you know your personality type, your communication style, and your conflict style. Recognizing your traits and patterns allows you an opportunity to choose careers, pick people, and engage in activities that bring out the best in you and minimize the worst of you. Instead of acting according to your comfort zone default, you can make choices that align with your strengths and values while still stretching you to be your best.

2. **Reading others:** With EQ, you can pay better attention to others and your environment. The golden rule is "Treat others the way you want to be treated"— but the EQ rule is "Treat others the way *they* want to be treated." As your empathy increases, you'll able to

connect to others by noticing how they respond. You'll gain a clearer understanding of what they need from their interactions with you. As you exit the comfort zone, you will benefit from the strength and support of healthy, high-functioning relationships.

3. **Responding appropriately:** Instead of allowing your preferred approach to dictate your behavior, you can use your EQ to gain self-control and make temporary adjustments that are usually a little uncomfortable but more effective. Those with higher EQ can frame the same message in several ways to meet the varying needs of others while also meeting their own needs. They manage their impulses so they don't have emotional outbursts or other inappropriate responses. Responding appropriately means matching your reactions to someone else, whether that involves opening yourself up or holding back—it's about showing your emotions appropriately, not about being emotion*less*. Using EQ to respond to others may involve stepping outside of your comfort zone. When you do, obstacles will disappear, people will work with you rather than against you, and the momentum will carry you into the confidence zone.

Let me explain through an example. When a former coworker of mine, Lauren, broke through several personal comfort barriers at work, she discovered she was capable of much more than she knew. She was working in the corporate communications department at her company, and after several years in the same role, the work was starting to feel mundane and routine. She could feel herself disengaging from her job: She no longer looked forward to going to work, and she had a hard time "giving her all" to her assignments.

After some self-reflection, Lauren realized that one of her favorite parts of her job was helping her team with their professional development. Since the organization didn't have a professional development division, she asked upper management to allow her to create the role and add it to her current duties.

Asking for this new position required Lauren to move into the discomfort zone in several ways: She had never held a learning and development role before, and the added new tasks would be piled on top of her current responsibilities. She would be taking on a big, highly visible project that could hurt her reputation if she failed. But Lauren faced her fears and mustered her courage to ask for the opportunity, and she got it. She says creating the new position wasn't easy, and her work didn't always go smoothly. But she remained open to learning as much as she could and made adaptations when things went wrong.

Ultimately, Lauren built a successful program, and after a few years, she was promoted to chief communications officer for her division. When she looks back at that time in her life, she knows that the confidence she gained from the experience propelled her to new and better opportunities. What's more, she says her life is so much richer and more satisfying now because she took the risk and built an interesting, challenging career for herself.

Throughout this book, I have tried to encourage you to take a deeper look at the patterns you've established in your life that are keeping you in your comfort zone. You can only reach your fullest potential when you let go of those habits that are no longer moving you forward and embrace new actions that push you toward your goals.

Letting go can also be an incredible release. The initial pain you feel when entering the discomfort zone may be transformed to excitement at discovering an entirely new direction in your life. I'm asking you to look beyond the confines of your comfort and embrace the potential of the expansion that awaits. No matter what happens to you as you move through your life, I hope you keep seeking out challenges and pushing yourself to spiral upward through the quadrants, so that you never stop growing. My story is not about luck. It is about not quitting.

Is There a Catfish in Your Life?

There's a parable told by spiritual leaders that serves as a great illustration for this kind of constant growth.[1] According to the story, fishermen on the East Coast of the United States typically flash-froze the cod they caught so it would stay fresh during shipment to the West Coast. However, their customers complained that when they thawed the fish to cook it, it was mushy and tasteless. Looking for a creative solution, the fishermen then tried shipping the cod by train, keeping them alive in large tanks, but still they found the cod arrived in poor eating condition.

Folklore says the natural predator of the cod is the catfish. So the fishermen started adding a few catfish to each shipment tank of cod to chase them around and keep them active on their journey. It turned out that when the cod traveled with catfish, they arrived firm and flavorful, which proved that the need to stay motivated did provide better results.

My question for you is, do you have a catfish in your life that keeps you thriving? Your catfish doesn't need to be a predator. It might be a colleague with whom you have a friendly competition, or a "frenemy"—someone whose friendship comes with just a touch of one-upmanship. It might be a pessimistic family member or an acquaintance who tends to be a naysayer about your dreams. Having someone like that in your life can be frustrating, but it can be useful, too, because it keeps you on your toes, always striving to do better.

Because my industry isn't a large one and there aren't a lot of women doing what I do, I've had to seek out people who keep me motivated. It took a while, but I found a couple, and the search has been worth it. Having a catfish or two chasing me around the tank makes me stronger and boots me out of my comfort zone on a regular basis.

For example, when I published my first book and it sold well, I was tempted to put down my pen and rest on my laurels. Writing doesn't come easily to me, and I had to put in a lot of hard work. I'd logged my time in the discomfort zone and made it into the confidence zone—now I just wanted to chill out in my comfort zone and rest.

I did rest, for a while. I took the time to recharge and to feel proud of myself for what I'd accomplished. I might have stayed cozily in my comfort zone, riding the wake of that one book, but after a while I began to feel my energy for challenge returning, and my EQ kicked in. I started to use the three *R*s as I looked around and read what was happening in my profession. What new topics had come to the fore? What issues were people struggling with, what questions kept coming up when I gave my talks?

When I took a read on the world around me, I found that the people I respected were writing second and third books. I'm a born competitor, so I couldn't stop with just one! If they could do it, so could I. So I picked that pen up again and stepped back into the discomfort zone—and you're holding the result in your hands, an accomplishment I can be proud of, that I might never have achieved without those catfish at my heels.

If you don't have a catfish of your own, I'd urge you to seek one out. Look for peers who challenge you, or even your own personal Lex Luthor who will keep you moving through the four quadrants and growing stronger and better with every cycle. I've found that there's a collegiality among women, so that even as we compete with each other, vying for the same jobs and recognitions, we lift each other up. The competition empowers all of us.

If you don't enjoy competition, you can still find a catfish or two in your life. Maybe it's that credit card debt that's been chasing you around the tank, or the master's degree that you are pushing yourself to finish. Maybe you can motivate yourself by making a promise to your loved ones that you'll quit smoking or lose weight, so you can live a long and happy life with them. A little healthy competition with yourself can be very inspiring and might provide just the motivation you need to take those first steps toward your confidence zone.

In Summary—Lean Into Your Power

Shortly after my marriage ended, when I was newly single and still adjusting, I noticed that invitations to parties and other social events had stopped coming in. If you've been divorced, you've probably experienced this too—friends you had as a couple feel uncomfortable inviting just one of you to a gathering. Maybe they want to avoid taking sides, or maybe they just don't like having a single person mixed in with the couples.

I was feeling lonely and blue about this one weekend, and I shared my feelings with my Grandma Irene. She had also divorced when her children were teenagers and spent the rest of her life single, so I knew she could relate.

I said, "I guess I understand why I wasn't invited; the women probably don't like having a single woman around their husbands."

She said, "More than likely, the husbands don't want you around their wives."

You grow in power and independence when you face your challenges. You no longer worry as much about risk or failure, because you know they'll help you grow even stronger. You learn that you have the strength to endure difficulties you never thought you could. You stop backing down under pressure or saying yes when you really want to say no. You look for the best in yourself and others, and you have the courage to walk away from those who demotivate you, bring negativity into your life, or stress you out. You reach more goals, achieve more dreams, and influence others more successfully, because people are drawn to those who are humble, hard-working, and positive.

Deep down, you probably know the one or two things you've been avoiding that would truly change your life—the things you're deliberately putting off thinking about. More than anything else, I'd love for you to start asking yourself what those things are. I hope that as you finish this book, you've gained a new understanding of where you are in the quadrants, and why. I hope you can look at your story and own it, and understand that you are the author. You have the power and resilience to decide what your next chapter will be. Make it a good one!

Endnote

1   Charles R. Swindoll, *Come Before Winter and Share My Hope* (Grand Rapids, MI: Zondervan, 1994).